Contents

P9-EDI-090

Skills:

Addition Facts to 10

Follow the animals to race through the problems.

Go this way.

$$\begin{array}{r} 2 \\ +3 \\ \hline \end{array}$$

$$\begin{array}{r} 4 \\ +1 \\ \hline \end{array}$$

$$\begin{array}{r} 1 \\ +5 \\ \hline \end{array}$$

$$\begin{array}{r} 5 \\ +4 \\ \hline \end{array}$$

$$\begin{array}{r} 1 \\ +4 \\ \hline \end{array}$$

$$\begin{array}{r} 2 \\ +4 \\ \hline \end{array}$$

$$\begin{array}{r} 5 \\ +0 \\ \hline \end{array}$$

$$\begin{array}{r} 2 \\ +2 \\ \hline \end{array}$$

$$\begin{array}{r} 4 \\ +2 \\ \hline \end{array}$$

$$\begin{array}{r} 4 \\ +6 \\ \hline \end{array}$$

$$\begin{array}{r} 5 \\ +2 \\ \hline \end{array}$$

$$\begin{array}{r} 7 \\ +2 \\ \hline \end{array}$$

$$\begin{array}{r} 5 \\ +5 \\ \hline \end{array}$$

$$\begin{array}{r} 4 \\ +3 \\ \hline \end{array}$$

$$\begin{array}{r} 4 \\ +4 \\ \hline \end{array}$$

$$\begin{array}{r} 3 \\ +7 \\ \hline \end{array}$$

$$\begin{array}{r} 3 \\ +2 \\ \hline \end{array}$$

$$\begin{array}{r} 0 \\ +3 \\ \hline \end{array}$$

$$\begin{array}{r} 3 \\ +5 \\ \hline \end{array}$$

$$\begin{array}{r} 4 \\ +5 \\ \hline \end{array}$$

Field Day Fun

©2005 by Evan-Moor Corp. • EMC 4546 • Math

Shot Put

Skills:

Solving Word Problems

Addition Facts to 18

Six contestants took part in a shot put contest.
Here are the scores after two throws.

Name	First Throw (yards)	Second Throw (yards)
Arnie Ape	6	9
Ian Iguana	6	7
Terry Toad	8	9
Mark Moose	5	4
Brittany Bear	7	8
Mary Mouse	6	6

Add the two throws for each contestant.
Write the totals on the chart.

Team Number	Name	Total Yards Thrown
1	Arnie	
	Ian	
2	Terry	
	Mark	
3	Brittany	
	Mary	

Which shot-putter had the most yards? _____

Which shot-putter had the least yards? _____

Which two shot-putters tied for the same number of yards?

_____   _____

Which team member had more total yards?

Team 1_____

Team 2_____

Team 3_____

Field Day Fun

Math • EMC 4546 • ©2005 by Evan-Moor Corp.

Skills:

Subtraction
Facts to 10

Solve each subtraction problem to help Robby Rabbit make it to the end of the race.

$$\begin{array}{r} 5 \\ -3 \\ \hline \end{array}$$
$$\begin{array}{r} 6 \\ -3 \\ \hline \end{array}$$
$$\begin{array}{r} 3 \\ -2 \\ \hline \end{array}$$
$$\begin{array}{r} 9 \\ -6 \\ \hline \end{array}$$
$$\begin{array}{r} 5 \\ -4 \\ \hline \end{array}$$
$$\begin{array}{r} 7 \\ -4 \\ \hline \end{array}$$

$$\begin{array}{r} 4 \\ -3 \\ \hline \end{array}$$
$$\begin{array}{r} 9 \\ -1 \\ \hline \end{array}$$
$$\begin{array}{r} 9 \\ -5 \\ \hline \end{array}$$
$$\begin{array}{r} 8 \\ -4 \\ \hline \end{array}$$

$$\begin{array}{r} 8 \\ -6 \\ \hline \end{array}$$
$$\begin{array}{r} 5 \\ -2 \\ \hline \end{array}$$
$$\begin{array}{r} 4 \\ -2 \\ \hline \end{array}$$
$$\begin{array}{r} 5 \\ -5 \\ \hline \end{array}$$

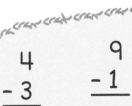

$$\begin{array}{r} 6 \\ -2 \\ \hline \end{array}$$
$$\begin{array}{r} 8 \\ -3 \\ \hline \end{array}$$
$$\begin{array}{r} 8 \\ -5 \\ \hline \end{array}$$
$$\begin{array}{r} 7 \\ -2 \\ \hline \end{array}$$

$$\begin{array}{r} 3 \\ -3 \\ \hline \end{array}$$
$$\begin{array}{r} 8 \\ -2 \\ \hline \end{array}$$
$$\begin{array}{r} 6 \\ -4 \\ \hline \end{array}$$
$$\begin{array}{r} 5 \\ -0 \\ \hline \end{array}$$
$$\begin{array}{r} 7 \\ -3 \\ \hline \end{array}$$
$$\begin{array}{r} 9 \\ -7 \\ \hline \end{array}$$

Finish

Field Day Fun

©2005 by Evan-Moor Corp. • EMC 4546 • Math

Running Out of Time

Skills:

Telling Time to the Half-hour

3:00      3:30

Write the times for each event.

100-Yard Dash	Shot Put	High Jump	The Mile Run

: _____	: _____	: _____	: _____

220-Yard Dash	Broad Jump	Hurdles	Relay Race

: _____	: _____	: _____	: _____

Draw the hands on the clocks.

50-Yard Dash	One-Mile Walk	Pole Vault	Triple Jump

9:00	11:00	5:30	12:30

Math • EMC 4546 • ©2005 by Evan-Moor Corp.

Field Day Fun

Skills:

Addition Facts
to 18

Follow the signs to get through the maze.

This way ———▶   **Sharp turn**

6	5	4	9	7	9
+ 7	+ 6	+ 7	+ 5	+ 5	+ 3

9	6	8	8	4	8
+ 6	+ 9	+ 8	+ 4	+ 8	+ 5

Hard left   ◀——— **Back this way**

Head for the tree

9	2	8	7	9	6
+ 9	+ 8	+ 3	+ 7	+ 7	+ 6

Last turn

You've made it out!

7	6	9	8	6	9
+ 6	+ 5	+ 4	+ 7	+ 8	+ 8

Field Day Fun

Randy Raccoon's Personal Best

Randy ran a mile every day for a week. He kept track of his times.

Day 1—16 minutes
Day 2—15 minutes, 45 seconds
Day 3—15 minutes, 45 seconds
Day 4—15 minutes, 30 seconds
Day 5—15 minutes, 45 seconds
Day 6—15 minutes, 15 seconds
Day 7—15 minutes

Show his times on the graph.

Times

	1	2	3	4	5	6	7
16 minutes							
15 minutes, 45 seconds							
15 minutes, 30 seconds							
15 minutes, 15 seconds							
15 minutes							

Days

Read the graph to answer the questions.

On which day did he have the best time? _____

On which day did he have the worst time? _____

On which three days did he have the same time?

_____   _____   _____

Field Day Fun

Skills:
Subtraction Facts
to 18

Dudley Dog needs help to find the finish line. Color all the squares with the same answer as Dudley's number.

12 − 7	16 − 7	13 − 5	14 − 7	17 − 8	15 − 9
13 − 8	11 − 6	14 − 9	10 − 5	13 − 9	12 − 9
14 − 5	12 − 5	16 − 9	11 − 6	12 − 7	14 − 9
18 − 9	11 − 8	13 − 7	17 − 9	16 − 8	13 − 8

©2005 by Evan-Moor Corp. • EMC 4546 • Math

UNIT 1

9

Field Day Fun

Skills:

Counting to Hundreds

Fill in the missing numbers to run the race.

Start

40	69	97	111	357
41	70	98	112	358
42	71	99	☐	359
☐	72	100	☐	☐
☐	73	☐	115	☐
45	☐	102	116	☐
46	☐	☐	☐	☐
47	76	104	118	364
48	77	105	☐	365
☐	☐	106	☐	☐
50	☐	☐	121	☐
51	80	108	122	368
52	81	☐	123	369
☐	☐	☐	124	370
☐	☐	111	☐	371

Finish

Field Day Fun

10   UNIT 1

Math • EMC 4546 • ©2005 by Evan-Moor Corp.

Skills:

Writing Number
Sentences

Each contestant tossed a ball two times. Write the equation.

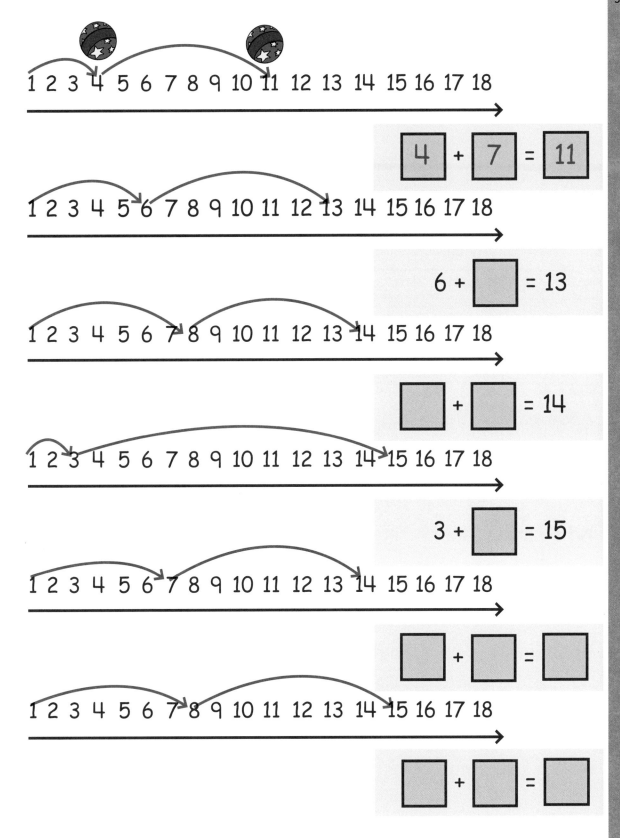

$4 + 7 = 11$

$6 + \boxed{} = 13$

$\boxed{} + \boxed{} = 14$

$3 + \boxed{} = 15$

$\boxed{} + \boxed{} = \boxed{}$

$\boxed{} + \boxed{} = \boxed{}$

Field Day Fun

The Finish Line

The same six contestants had a race.
The times of the race are given on the chart.

Name	Time on Stopwatch
Arnie Ape	9 minutes
Ian Iguana	8 minutes
Terry Toad	7 minutes
Mark Moose	4 minutes
Brittany Bear	6 minutes
Mary Mouse	5 minutes

Answer the questions.

Who won the race? _____

Who came in last? _____

Who came in second? _____

Who finished one minute before Ian? _____

Who finished four minutes after Mary? _____

How many minutes faster was Mark than Mary? _____

Field Day Fun

Robbie Rabbit entered every running event. After you solve the problems, color all the boxes in which the answers are 9 or 14 to see how many races Robbie won.

9 + 9	8 + 6	7 + 6	5 + 9	14 − 7	12 − 8
8 + 5	18 − 9	15 − 7	7 + 7	16 − 8	6 + 6
8 + 8	13 − 4	15 − 6	16 − 7	17 − 8	9 + 7
17 − 9	5 + 7	7 + 8	9 + 5	16 − 9	15 − 9
18 − 8	11 − 8	15 − 8	12 − 3	16 − 8	12 − 9

Robbie won _____ races.

©2005 by Evan-Moor Corp. • EMC 4546 • Math

Field Day Fun

TEST YOUR SKILLS

Add or subtract.

Fill in the circle for the correct answer.

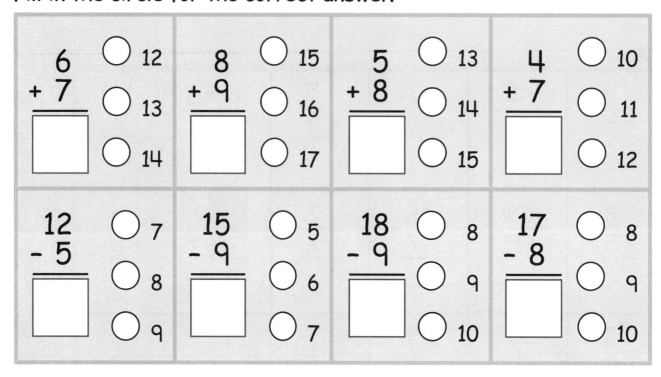

6 + 7	○ 12 ○ 13 ○ 14
8 + 9	○ 15 ○ 16 ○ 17
5 + 8	○ 13 ○ 14 ○ 15
4 + 7	○ 10 ○ 11 ○ 12

12 − 5	○ 7 ○ 8 ○ 9
15 − 9	○ 5 ○ 6 ○ 7
18 − 9	○ 8 ○ 9 ○ 10
17 − 8	○ 8 ○ 9 ○ 10

Write the time.

: _____   : _____   : _____   : _____

What's missing?

43	44	☐	☐	47	☐	49	☐
98	99	☐	☐	102	103	☐	
364	365	☐	☐	368	369	☐	

Math • EMC 4546 • ©2005 by Evan-Moor Corp.

Skills:

Column Addition

When you add three or more numbers, it's easier to add pairs of numbers first.

$$
\begin{array}{cc}
5 \rangle & 9 \\
4 & \\
2 \rangle & 8 \\
+\,6 & +\,9 \\
\hline
& 17
\end{array}
$$

$$
\begin{array}{l}
2 \rangle \;\square \\
4 \\
2 \rangle \;+\; \square \\
+\,3 \\
\hline
\quad 11
\end{array}
\qquad
\begin{array}{l}
2 \rangle \;\square \\
7 \\
2 \rangle \;+\; \square \\
+\,5 \\
\hline
\quad 16
\end{array}
\qquad
\begin{array}{l}
1 \rangle \;\square \\
6 \\
3 \rangle \;+\; \square \\
+\,2 \\
\hline
\quad 12
\end{array}
$$

$$
\begin{array}{l}
2 \rangle \;\square \\
7 \\
7 \rangle \;+\; \square \\
+\,3 \\
\hline
\quad \square
\end{array}
\qquad
\begin{array}{l}
6 \rangle \;\square \\
2 \\
2 \rangle \;+\; \square \\
+\,6 \\
\hline
\quad \square
\end{array}
\qquad
\begin{array}{l}
5 \rangle \;\square \\
4 \\
3 \rangle \;+\; \square \\
+\,3 \\
\hline
\quad \square
\end{array}
$$

$$
\begin{array}{l}
6 \rangle \;\square \\
1 \\
3 \rangle \;+\; \square \\
+\,3 \\
\hline
\quad \square
\end{array}
\qquad
\begin{array}{l}
4 \rangle \;\square \\
4 \\
2 \rangle \;+\; \square \\
+\,2 \\
\hline
\quad \square
\end{array}
\qquad
\begin{array}{l}
3 \rangle \;\square \\
4 \\
4 \rangle \;+\; \square \\
+\,3 \\
\hline
\quad \square
\end{array}
$$

At the Market

Enough Money?

Example: Jan is going to the store. She has 15¢. She wants to buy two pieces of candy. The candy costs 7¢ each. Does she have enough money?

___yes___   Show why. _7 + 7 = 14; 14 is less than 15_

Ryan has 18¢. He wants to buy three cookies. Each cookie costs 6¢. Does he have enough money?

_____ Show why. _____

Crystal has 14¢. She wants to buy 4 gumballs. Each gumball costs 4¢. Does she have enough money?

_____ Show why. _____

Chris wants to buy 2 packs of baseball cards. Each pack costs 10¢. He only has 18¢. How much more money does he need?

_____ Show why. _____

John wants to buy 4 jawbreakers. He has 10¢. Each jawbreaker costs 3¢. How much more money does he need?

_____ Show why. _____

Jill wants to buy 5 suckers. Each sucker costs 5¢. She has a quarter. Does she have enough money?

_____ Show why. _____

Math • EMC 4546 • ©2005 by Evan-Moor Corp.

At the Market

Skills:

Column Addition

Here's another way to solve column addition problems—Look for the two numbers that add up to 10.

Add.

```
  5
  4  ⟩10
  2      4     10
+ 5    + 2   + 6
              16
```

4	4	4	3
4	7	4	7
6	2	2	3
+ 2	+ 3	+ 6	+ 3

2	2	5	1
5	1	1	5
3	1	9	1
+ 5	+ 8	+ 2	+ 5

6	7	8	5
5	7	6	4
1	3	2	4
+ 4	+ 3	+ 2	+ 5

At the Market

©2005 by Evan-Moor Corp. • EMC 4546 • Math

Skills:

Number Words

Match each numeral to the number word.

 4 pounds • • twelve

 14 ounces • • twenty-eight

 12 ounces • • seven

 5 pounds • • forty-nine

 28 ounces • • four

 7 pounds • • eighteen

 18 pounds • • five

 49 ounces • • fourteen

At the Market

Math • EMC 4546 • ©2005 by Evan-Moor Corp.

Skills:

Column
Addition

Solve the problems.
Match each problem with the correct number.

```
  7
  1
  5
+ 3
____
```

```
  9
  4
  4
+ 1
____
```

```
  6
  2
  6
+ 3
____
```

```
  4
  6
  2
  6
+ 4
____
```

```
  5
  7
  5
+ 4
____
```

```
  2
  4
  2
  3
+ 1
____
```

```
  1
  3
  4
  2
  3
+ 1
____
```

```
  4
  6
  6
+ 4
____
```

At the Market

Money Counts

How much money is in each set of coins?

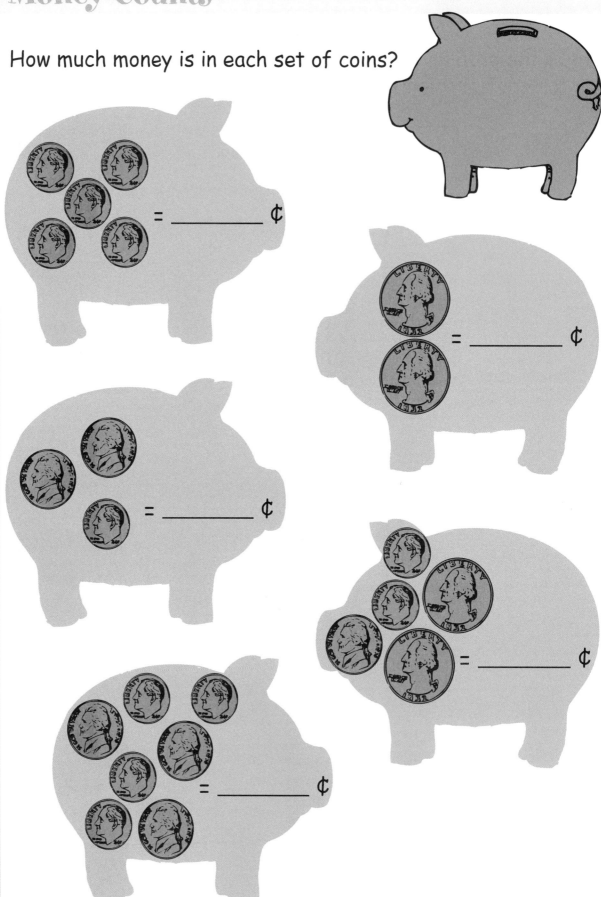

= _____ ¢

= _____ ¢

= _____ ¢

= _____ ¢

= _____ ¢

At the Market

Percy's Purchases

Percy needs to buy 60 ounces of peanuts. Each bag of peanuts holds 10 ounces. How many bags should he buy?

___6___ bags of peanuts

Show why.

```
  10
  10
  10
  10
  10
+ 10
────
  60
```

Percy needs to buy 40 ounces of beans. Each bag holds 10 ounces. How many bags should he buy?

_____ bags of beans

Show why.

Percy needs to buy 70 ounces of sunflower seeds. Each bag holds 10 ounces. How many bags should he buy?

_____ bags of seeds

Show why.

Percy needs to buy 80 ounces of peanut butter. Each jar holds 20 ounces. How many jars should he buy?

_____ jars of peanut butter

Show why.

At the Market

Skills:

Place Value—
Tens and Ones

10 ones = 1 ten

Count the tens and ones. Tell how many apples.

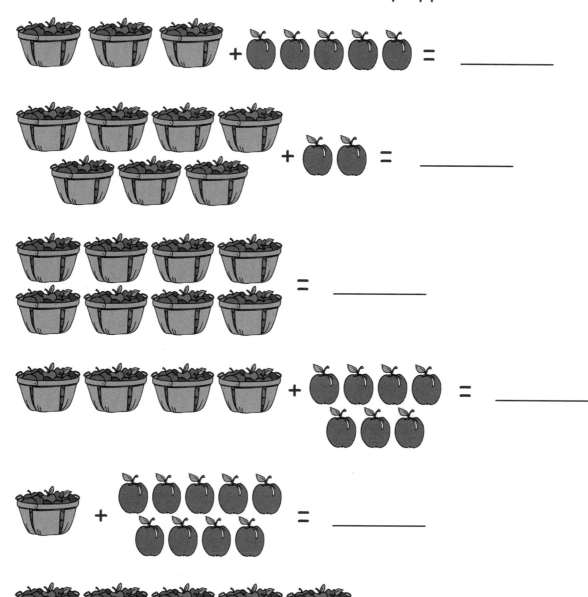

Math • EMC 4546 • ©2005 by Evan-Moor Corp.

Farmer Jones's Roadside Stand

Farmer Jones uses a pie graph to record the fruits and vegetables he sells each day at his roadside stand. Here is his graph for last Thursday. Read the graph. Answer the questions.

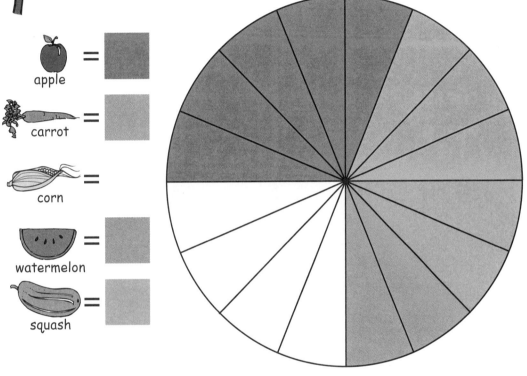

apple =

carrot =

corn =

watermelon =

squash =

1. How many carrots were sold? _____

2. Which food sold the most? _____

3. How many more ears of corn than squash were sold? _____

4. Which food was $\frac{1}{4}$ of the total amount sold on Thursday? _____

At the Market

©2005 by Evan-Moor Corp. • EMC 4546 • Math

UNIT 2

23

Check It Out!

Skills:

Adding and
Subtracting
Money

Add the items at the check-out counter.
Then use your cents-off coupon.

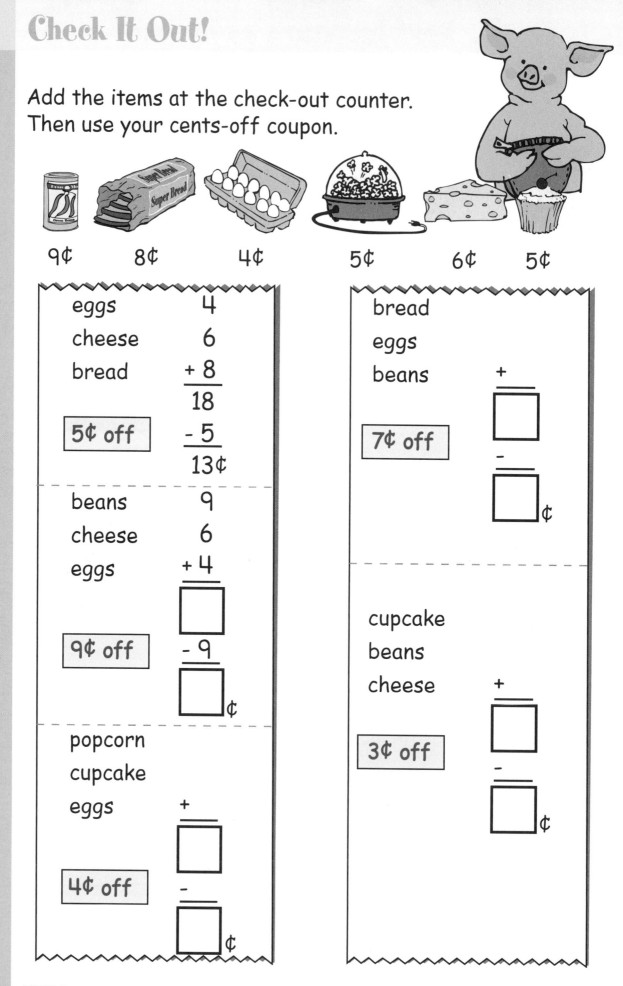

At the Market

9¢   8¢   4¢   5¢   6¢   5¢

eggs	4
cheese	6
bread	+ 8
	18
5¢ off	- 5
	13¢

beans	9
cheese	6
eggs	+ 4
	☐
9¢ off	- 9
	☐ ¢

popcorn	
cupcake	
eggs	+
	☐
4¢ off	-
	☐ ¢

bread	
eggs	
beans	+
	☐
7¢ off	-
	☐ ¢

cupcake	
beans	
cheese	+
	☐
3¢ off	-
	☐ ¢

Math • EMC 4546 • ©2005 by Evan-Moor Corp.

Picking a Peck of Peppers

Patty Pig picks peppers to sell at the Peppy Boys Market. She uses tally marks to keep track of the peppers she picks. Help Patty track her peppers.

ℍ = 5

Week One	Tally	How Many?
Monday	IIII	4
Tuesday	ℍ IIII	___
Wednesday	ℍ ℍ	___
Thursday	ℍ II	___
Friday	ℍ I	___

Week Two	Tally	How Many?
Monday	ℍ ℍ I	___
Tuesday	ℍ II	___
Wednesday	ℍ ℍ ℍ	___
Thursday	ℍ II	___
Friday	ℍ ℍ ℍ II	___

Patty earns 1¢ for each pepper she picks.

How much did she earn in Week One? _____

In which week did she earn more money? _____

How much more? _____

Skills:

Using Tally Marks

Solving Word Problems

How Long Is That Zucchini?

There are zucchinis of all sizes in the squash bin.

Measure them.

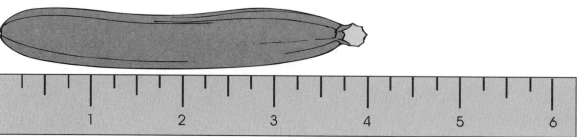

_____ inches

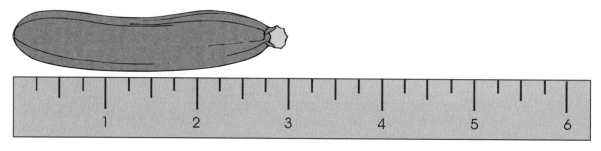

_____ inches

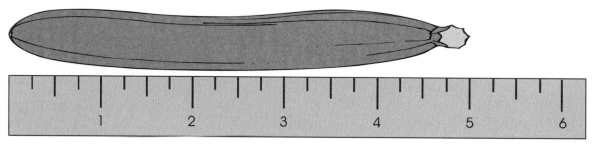

_____ inches

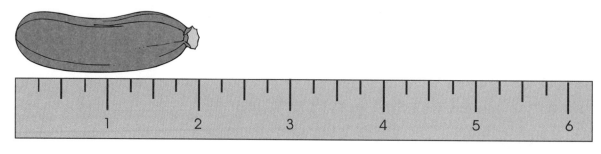

_____ inches

At the Market

Math • EMC 4546 • ©2005 by Evan-Moor Corp.

TEST YOUR SKILLS

Add or subtract.

5	8	9	7	6	7
+4	+6	+0	+9	+6	+8
☐	☐	☐	☐	☐	☐

```
 3        1
 6        9
 5        3
+5       +3
 ☐        ☐
```

14	10	13	14	15	18
−9	−8	−4	−7	−8	−9
☐	☐	☐	☐	☐	☐

What is the time?

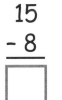

_____:_____   _____:_____

How much money?

= _____¢

What's missing?

98 99 ☐ ☐ 102 ☐

☐ ☐ 361 ☐ ☐

Match.

卌 卌 II •   • 16

twenty-seven •   • 19

sixteen •   • 12

卌 卌 卌 IIII •   • 27

How long?

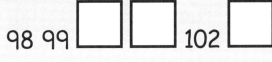

2 inches   8 inches   4 inches

Sally bought a banana for 6¢, an orange for 4¢, and an apple for 8¢. How much did she spend? _____

©2005 by Evan-Moor Corp. • EMC 4546 • Math

What's Cooking?

Skills:

Two-Digit
Addition
Without
Regrouping

When you add 2-digit numbers, be sure to add the **ones** column first.

Find all the answers that have 9 in the **ones** place. Write the letters of those problems in order on the blank lines. Then you will know what's cooking!

tens	ones
1	4
+2	3
3	7

a	j	m	d	s	r	g
21	11	23	33	35	21	30
+ 5	+ 7	+ 12	+ 45	+ 14	+ 26	+ 8

h	t	b	v	l	c	n
52	16	63	55	32	91	44
+ 14	+ 23	+ 15	+ 12	+ 26	+ 3	+ 44

u	p	y	f	e	i	o
62	77	63	80	21	15	74
+ 24	+ 21	+ 33	+ 11	+ 48	+ 11	+ 23

k	w	x	q	z
34	22	64	24	42
+ 32	+ 37	+ 20	+ 71	+ 35

_____ _____ _____ _____ _____

Math • EMC 4546 • ©2005 by Evan-Moor Corp.

In the Kitchen

Skills:

Two-Digit
Subtraction
Without
Regrouping

Chef Louis has created a wonderful surprise for dessert. Shade each square where the answer has 6 in the **tens** place. This will tell you the first letter of the surprise. Then circle the picture of the surprise dessert.

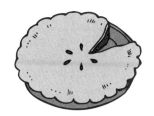

69 - 36	79 - 15	87 - 23	96 - 33	88 - 24	47 - 12
77 - 52	95 - 35	39 - 14	87 - 54	68 - 6	90 - 60
99 - 86	87 - 25	78 - 15	74 - 12	99 - 35	72 - 41
96 - 71	67 - 7	66 - 33	68 - 55	97 - 63	88 - 64
75 - 62	82 - 20	98 - 24	99 - 4	40 - 20	56 - 25
68 - 27	77 - 11	83 - 42	80 - 40	59 - 49	58 - 17

©2005 by Evan-Moor Corp. • EMC 4546 • Math

In the Kitchen

Skills:

Addition
Without
Regrouping

Telling Time to
the Half-hour

Cookies, Cookies, and More Cookies

Help Baker Bob know how many cookies he can make. Fill in the table.

One Batch	Two Batches	Three Batches	Four Batches
20			
30			120
40		120	
12			
21			

It takes one-half hour to bake a big tray of cookies. Write the time each tray of cookies will be done.

1:30

:

:

:

:

:

In the Kitchen

30

UNIT 3

Math • EMC 4546 • ©2005 by Evan-Moor Corp.

Busy Bakers

Write each problem and then solve it.

Ann's cookie recipe makes 12 cookies.
If she makes a double batch,
how many cookies will she have?

_____ cookies

Fred made two cookies for each
of his kids. He has three kids.
How many cookies did Fred make?

_____ cookies

Bob had 10 eggs.
He used 4 eggs to make bread.
He used 2 eggs to make cookies.
How many eggs does he have left?

_____ eggs

Jill baked this cake.
Show how she cut the cake
for eight people. Make each
piece the same size.

Jerry bought 3 dozen donuts.
How many donuts does he have?

(hint: 1 dozen = 12)

_____ donuts

In the Kitchen

Measure It!

Measure the milk. Color to show the right amount.

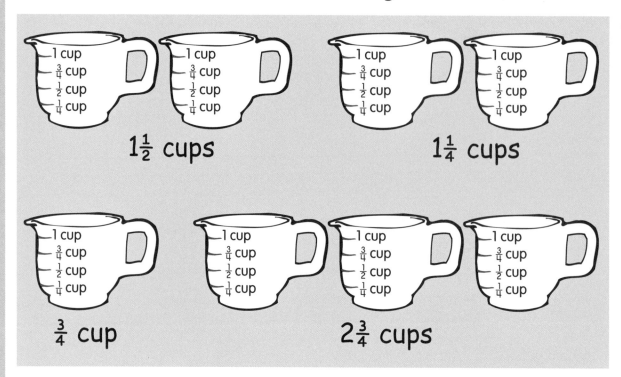

Measure the butter. Color to show the right amount.

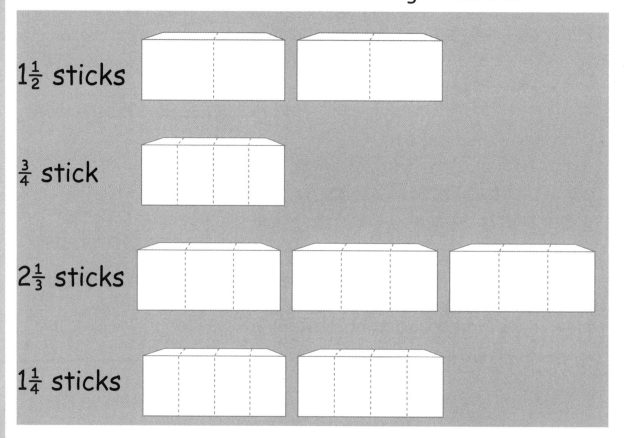

In the Kitchen

Healthy Hillary is looking for a snack. She wants to keep her snack under 250 calories because she will have a big dinner later.

Add up the calories in each snack. Then circle each snack that Hillary might choose.

200 calories

10 calories

20 calories

104 calories

80 calories

100 calories

Yum!

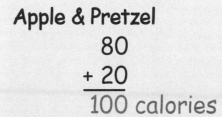

Apple & Pretzel

    80
+ 20
────────
  100 calories

Hot Dog & Ice Cream

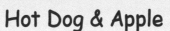

Peanut Butter & Celery

Hot Dog & Apple

Ice Cream, Apple, & Celery

In the Kitchen

Pizza Fractions

$\frac{1}{2}$ = one of 2 equal parts $\frac{1}{3}$ = one of 3 equal parts

$\frac{1}{4}$ = one of 4 equal parts $\frac{1}{8}$ = one of 8 equal parts

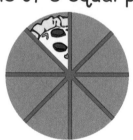

Color to show the fraction.

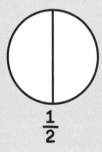   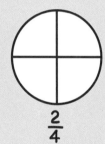   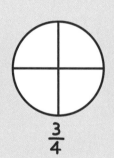   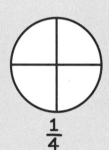

$\frac{1}{2}$ $\frac{2}{4}$ $\frac{3}{4}$ $\frac{1}{4}$

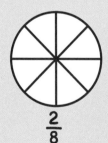   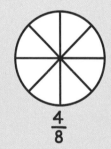   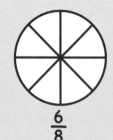   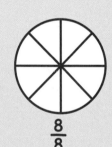

$\frac{2}{8}$ $\frac{4}{8}$ $\frac{6}{8}$ $\frac{8}{8}$

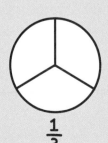   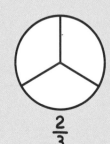

$\frac{1}{3}$ $\frac{2}{3}$ $\frac{3}{3}$

34   UNIT 3   Math • EMC 4546 • ©2005 by Evan-Moor Corp.

In the Kitchen

What's the Secret Ingredient?

Add.

K	A	O	I	N	F
155 + 21	72 + 27	103 + 95	362 + 17	560 + 15	200 + 76

Y	A	N	D	C	D
904 + 13	303 + 55	42 + 33	88 + 10	543 + 33	43 + 21

I	T	O	N	G	I
176 + 10	404 + 51	654 + 13	711 + 32	100 + 99	155 + 11

T	W	O	U	R	S
77 + 10	17 + 42	111 + 23	234 + 55	19 + 20	30 + 49

Write the letter that goes with each answer to find the secret ingredient.

___ ___ ___ ___ ___ ___ ___ ___ ___ ___ ___

176 75 198 59 379 575 199   917 134 289 39

___ ___ ___ ___ ___ ___ ___ ___ ___ ___ ___ ___ ___

99 98 64 186 455 166 667 743   276 358 576 87 79

In the Kitchen

©2005 by Evan-Moor Corp. • EMC 4546 • Math

Family Favorites

Alex surveyed his family to find out
what foods were their favorites.
He marked each food that a person liked.

	Pizza	Hamburger	Taco	Stir Fry	Hot Dog
Mom	X			X	
Dad	X	X	X		X
Cleo	X	X			
Alex	X	X	X	X	X
Malcolm	X		X	X	

Use the chart to complete this graph.

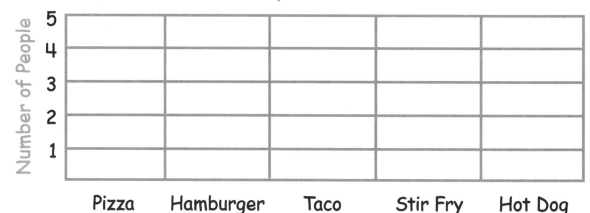

Family Favorites

Answer these questions about the graph.

What food does everyone like? _____

What food do the fewest people like? _____

Which foods have the same number of votes?

_____ _____ _____

Which of the foods on the graph is your favorite?

_____

Cookie Fractions

$\frac{1}{2}$ < $\frac{3}{4}$

Color the correct number of cookies.
Use >, <, or = to compare the amounts.

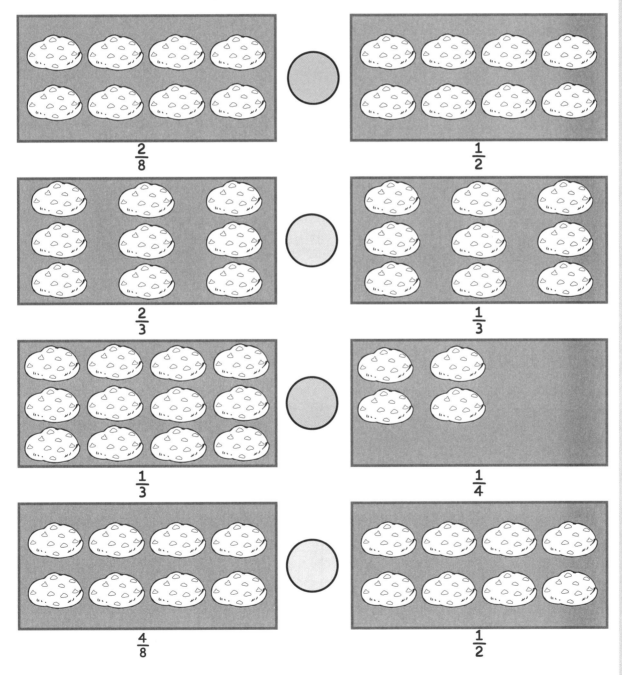

$\frac{2}{8}$ $\frac{1}{2}$

$\frac{2}{3}$ $\frac{1}{3}$

$\frac{1}{3}$ $\frac{1}{4}$

$\frac{4}{8}$ $\frac{1}{2}$

In the Kitchen

What Did You Eat?

Your meal cost $8.00. What did you eat?

Menu

Hot Dog	$4.00	Hamburger	$5.00
Sandwich	$7.00	Chips	$1.00

sandwich and chips

Show your work.

$7.00
+ $1.00
$8.00

Your meal cost $10.00. What did you eat?

Menu

Pizza	$7.00	Drink	$2.00
Salad	$3.00	Ice Cream	$4.00

Show your work.

Your meal cost $12.00. What did you eat?

Menu

Taco	$2.00	Burrito	$3.00
Corn Chips	$1.00	Nachos	$7.00

Show your work.

Math • EMC 4546 • ©2005 by Evan-Moor Corp.

In the Kitchen

Add or subtract.
Fill in the circle to show the answer.

35
+24
⬚
○ 69
○ 59
○ 49

21
+47
⬚
○ 67
○ 68
○ 69

67
+22
⬚
○ 45
○ 59
○ 89

69
-36
⬚
○ 34
○ 33
○ 95

47
-23
⬚
○ 24
○ 80
○ 69

64
-51
⬚
○ 18
○ 15
○ 13

Color to show the correct amount.

1½ sticks

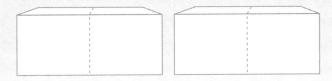

1¾ cups

Draw a line to make a match.

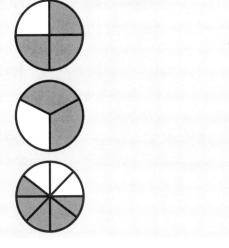

$\frac{5}{8}$

$\frac{3}{4}$

$\frac{2}{3}$

Your meal cost $8.00.
What did you eat?

Menu	
hot dog $4.00	chips $1.00
hamburger $5.00	soda $2.00

_____
_____
_____

©2005 by Evan-Moor Corp. • EMC 4546 • Math

Skills:

Subtraction
Facts

Two-Digit
Subtraction

Why do ducks have big bills?

Subtract.

24	45	98	35	64	76
− 4	− 11	− 37	− 10	− 54	− 44
20					

88	51	17	12	16	14
− 44	− 21	− 9	− 6	− 9	− 5

Circle the word beside each answer you find below. You will not find all the answers. Read the circled words from top to bottom.

1 Ducks	20 (Because)	4 They	33 The
0 run	3 for	18 the	9 they
6 buy	21 go	5 have	19 big
2 and	10 a	40 of	22 to
14 hot	15 fun	34 lot	38 done

Fun and Games

Skills:
Symmetry

If you draw a line through the middle of something and both sides are the same, the object is symmetrical.

Draw to make the pictures symmetrical.

Fun and Games

Can You Believe Your Eyes?

Skills:

Three-Digit
Subtraction
Without
Regrouping

Color answers that **end** in:

0 green	2 purple	4 red
1 blue	3 violet	5 orange

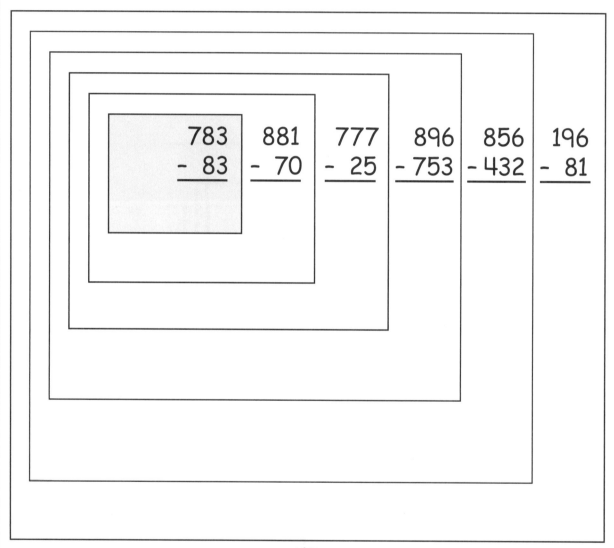

```
 783    881    777    896    856    196
- 83   - 70   - 25   -753   -432   - 81
```

Math • EMC 4546 • ©2005 by Evan-Moor Corp.

Fun and Games

Skills:

Counting by 2s, 5s, and 10s

Lizzie, Sam, and Missy each took a different path at the amusement park.

Lizzie took the counting-by-tens path.
Sam took the counting-by-fives path.
Missy took the counting-by-twos path.

Color the 10s path red. Color the 5s path blue. Color the 2s path green.

Write each name beside the ride where his or her path led.

Missy   Sam   Lizzie

2	9	11	25	5	10	18	10	7	23
4	6	8	27	29	15	19	20	9	29
21	25	10	30	25	20	21	30	11	30
23	27	12	14	30	35	40	40	13	120
22	20	18	16	31	32	45	50	17	110
24	33	13	33	60	55	50	60	18	100
29	3	17	3	65	13	25	70	80	90

bumper cars

Ferris wheel

merry-go-round

_____

©2005 by Evan-Moor Corp. • EMC 4546 • Math

Fun and Games

Basketball Pointers

Skills:

Solving Word Problems

Write each problem. Then solve it.

The Bulldog basketball team ended the game with 76 points. The Tigers had 66 points. By how many points did the Bulldogs win?

_____

The Lions had 46 points at the end of the game. They made 24 points in the first half. How many points did they make in the second half?

_____

The Bulldogs played nine players in the first half and eight different players in the second half. How many Bulldogs played in the game?

_____

The Tigers' score was 24. That score was 64 points less than the Bulldogs' score. What was the Bulldogs' score?

_____

The Bulldogs bought three new basketballs for the game. Each ball cost $20.00. How much did the team spend?

_____

The clock showed 55 seconds left in the game. The next play took 32 seconds. How many seconds were left in the game?

_____

Fun and Games

Math • EMC 4546 • ©2005 by Evan-Moor Corp.

Cowboy Dan is fixin' to lasso up some money to buy some new duds.

Circle the amount of money needed to buy each thing.

$5.55

$1.25

$2.35

$4.75

©2005 by Evan-Moor Corp. • EMC 4546 • Math

A Goofy Riddle

What can you wear that everyone will like?

A – 24	E – 22	G – 53	R – 45
B – 35	I – 12	N – 16	T – 17

$$87 - 63 = \boxed{}$$

$$68 - 15 = \boxed{} \quad 89 - 44 = \boxed{} \quad 59 - 37 = \boxed{} \quad 78 - 54 = \boxed{} \quad 78 - 61 = \boxed{}$$

$$69 - 34 = \boxed{} \quad 74 - 62 = \boxed{} \quad 99 - 46 = \boxed{}$$

$$87 - 34 = \boxed{} \quad 56 - 11 = \boxed{} \quad 48 - 36 = \boxed{} \quad 99 - 83 = \boxed{}$$

Draw the answer here.

Fun and Games

Explorer Ed must cross a river full of hungry crocodiles. He could jump from rock to rock. But what if one of those rocks is really a crocodile?

Luckily, Ed knows that the **even-numbered** answers are **rocks**. The odd-numbered answers are not rocks, but crocodiles.

Even numbers, counting by 2s: 2, 4, 6, 8, 10, and so on

Odd numbers: 1, 3, 5, 7, 9, 11, and so on

Solve each problem. Then color the safe route for Explorer Ed.

14 – 6 = 8

15 – 8 =

12 – 8 =

6 + 6 =

9 + 8 =

10 – 6 =

16 – 8 =

9 + 7 =

7 + 5 =

8 + 7 =

18 – 9 =

14 – 8 =

7 + 5 =

7 + 6 =

Bull's-Eye

Play this game by yourself or with a friend.

Rules for One:

Drop a coin 2 times on the target.
Add the numbers.
If your score is more than 50, you win.

Rules for Two:

Take turns.
Drop a coin 2 times.
Add the numbers.
The highest score wins.

Fun and Games

Skills:

Solving Word Problems

Three football players made these points: 3, 7, 21
Ron made the most points.
Mike made more points than Fred.
How many points did Fred make?

	3	7	21
Ron			X
Mike		X	
Fred	X		

<u>Fred made 3 points.</u>

Four soccer players made these goals: 0, 1, 2, 3
Joann made one goal.
Heather made twice as many goals
  as Joann.
Mandy made one more goal than
  Heather.
How many goals did Angela make?

	0	1	2	3
Heather				
Joann				
Mandy				
Angela				

_____

Three football players made these points: 6, 12, 18
John made the most points.
Gerry made half of what Bob made.
How many points did Bob make?

	6	12	18
John			
Gerry			
Bob			

_____

Five basketball players made these points: 10, 12, 12, 14, 20
Jane made the fewest points.
Debra made twice as many points
  as Jane.
Katie and Julie each made two more
  points than Jane.
How many points did Susan make?

	10	12	14	20
Katie				
Julie				
Debra				
Susan				
Jane				

_____

Fun and Games

Tick-Tock, Very Odd Clocks

Skills:

Telling Time to the Quarter Hour

When the minute hand is on the 9, it is 45 minutes past the hour.

8:45

When the minute hand is on the 3, it is 15 minutes past the hour.

7:15

Write the time shown on each clock.

_____ : _____   _____ : _____   _____ : _____   _____ : _____

_____ : _____   _____ : _____   _____ : _____   _____ : _____

_____ : _____   _____ : _____   _____ : _____   _____ : _____

Fun and Games

It Marks the Spot

Color the answers that **end** in **3** red.

433 - 100	404 - 300	995 - 870	556 - 401	887 - 343	345 - 12
999 - 405	275 - 252	555 - 341	756 - 752	456 - 123	779 - 505
665 - 660	777 - 543	507 - 104	567 - 234	708 - 404	567 - 222
888 - 123	386 - 222	678 - 345	914 - 801	997 - 303	668 - 663
587 - 543	789 - 456	695 - 341	446 - 132	339 - 126	554 - 110
456 - 123	854 - 330	449 - 434	568 - 63	657 - 223	828 - 525

What marks the spot? _____

Fun and Games

©2005 by Evan-Moor Corp. • EMC 4546 • Math

TEST YOUR SKILLS

Add or subtract.

21	33	72	58	68	226
+ 17	+ 44	+ 27	− 36	− 34	+ 102

Show ¼ of the set.

□ □ □ □

What fraction is colored?

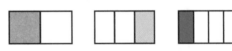

____   ____   ____

Read the graph.

Cookies

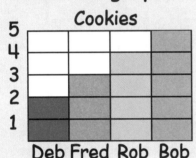

Deb Fred Rob Bob

Who ate the most? _____

Who had two less than Rob? _____

How many did Fred eat? _____

Circle $1.42.

What time is it?

Are both sides the same?

Yes   No

Circle the odd numbers.
Box the even numbers.

6   11   13   4

9   12   14   7

Count by 2s: ___12___, _____, _____, _____, _____

Count by 5s: ___15___, _____, _____, _____, _____

Skills:

Two-Digit
Addition with
Regrouping

If the **ones** place adds up to more than 9, you must **regroup**. That means you move the **tens** to the **tens place**.

Here's how:

```
   16          1            1
 + 16         16           16
             + 16         + 16
 _____       _____        _____
               2           32
```

Add the **ones**.   Write the ones. Move the tens to the tens place.   Add the **tens**.

Solve the problems.

```
    M           I           A           T
   18          33          57          44
  + 8        + 29        + 18        + 28
 _____       _____       _____       _____


    S           F           Y           U
   65          29          15          77
 + 15        + 29        + 68        + 13
 _____       _____       _____       _____


    W           O           R           D
   19          38          16          54
 + 47        + 38        + 26        + 19
 _____       _____       _____       _____
```

Write the letter for each answer below to find out when it will rain.

___ ___ ___ ___ ___ ___
58   42   62   73   75   83

Weather Watch

Skills:

Measurement—
Temperature

Weather Watch

Use the thermometer to help you decide what to wear.

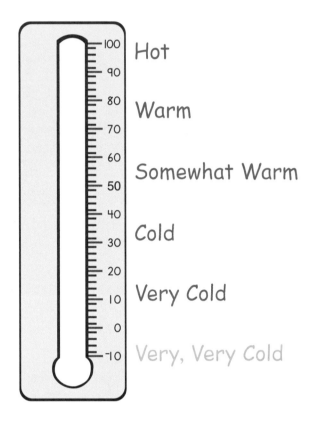

Hot

Warm

Somewhat Warm

Cold

Very Cold

Very, Very Cold

It's 10°F.

It's 40°F.

It's 65°F.

It's 100°F.

How Much Did It Snow?

Remember to add the **ones** first. Write the **ones** in the **ones** place; move the **tens** to the **tens** place.

Tens	Ones
1	

```
  4 7
+ 2 7
-----
  7 4
```

```
  73
+  9
```

```
  57
+ 23
```

```
  44
+  7
```

```
  64
+  9
```

```
  74
+ 19
```

```
  45
+ 36
```

```
  28
+ 46
```

```
  17
+ 47
```

```
  39
+  8
```

```
  52
+ 29
```

```
  44
+ 16
```

```
  26
+ 46
```

Circle the largest number in the **tens** place.
That will tell you how many inches it snowed.

It snowed _____ inches.

Weather Watch

Let It Snow!

Weather Watch

Write the problems. Then solve them.

1
It began snowing at 2:00 in the afternoon. At 8:00 that night it stopped. How many hours did it snow?

_____

2
If it snowed 2 inches every hour, how many inches of snow were there at 8:00?

_____

3
There were 28 children at the sledding hill. There were 18 sleds. How many children did **not** have a sled?

_____

4
The sledding hill is 220 feet long. How many feet will I sled if I go down the hill three times?

_____

5
My friends and I built 3 snow people. Each snow person was decorated with 2 sticks, 1 hat, and 4 buttons. How many of each thing did we use in all?

sticks   _____

hats   _____

buttons _____

6
The snow made it hard to drive on the roads. The news report said that 36 cars and 17 trucks had gotten stuck in the snow. How many vehicles got stuck?

_____

Math • EMC 4546 • ©2005 by Evan-Moor Corp.

Skills:

Counting by 2s
Reading a Thermometer

Count by 2s.

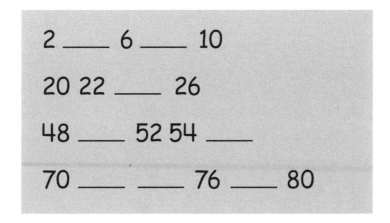

2 ___ 6 ___ 10

20 22 ___ 26

48 ___ 52 54 ___

70 ___ ___ 76 ___ 80

A Fahrenheit thermometer is usually marked in 2-degree units.

Read each thermometer and write the temperature.

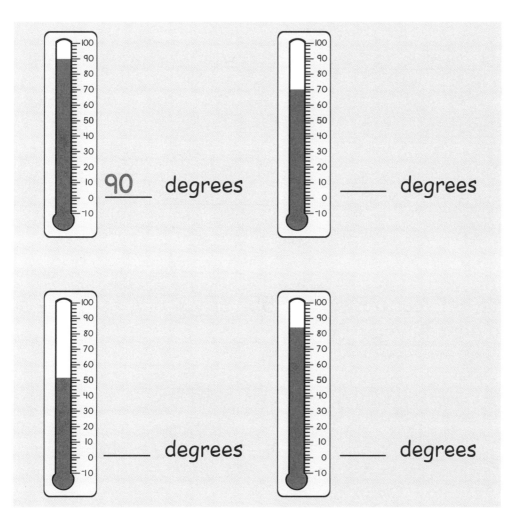

90 degrees

___ degrees

___ degrees

___ degrees

©2005 by Evan-Moor Corp. • EMC 4546 • Math

UNIT 5

57

Rain or Shine?

Add. Remember to add the ones first and then move any tens to the tens place.

$$17 + 7$$ $$15 + 9$$ $$18 + 8$$ $$14 + 9$$ $$19 + 9$$

$$17 + 38$$ $$19 + 15$$ $$19 + 53$$ $$29 + 26$$ $$36 + 19$$

$$28 + 35$$ $$19 + 75$$ $$17 + 24$$ $$18 + 37$$ $$34 + 57$$

Did you get four answers of 55? If you did, color the sun. If you did not, color the rain.

Weather Watch

Math • EMC 4546 • ©2005 by Evan-Moor Corp.

Color to show the fractions.

$\frac{1}{2}$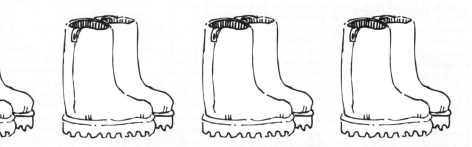

$\frac{1}{3}$

$\frac{1}{4}$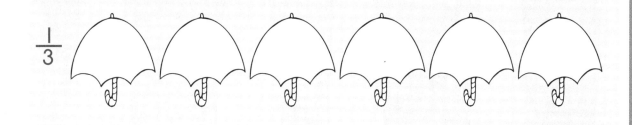

$\frac{2}{3}$

$\frac{3}{4}$

Weather Watch

How Long Are the Snowmen's Noses?

centimeters

0 1 2 3 4 5 6 7 8 9 10 11 12 13 14 15 16 17 18 19 20 21 22 23 24

Here are some carrots used to make noses for five snowmen. Cut out the centimeter ruler on the left side of the page and measure each carrot.

_____ cm   _____ cm   _____ cm   _____ cm   _____ cm

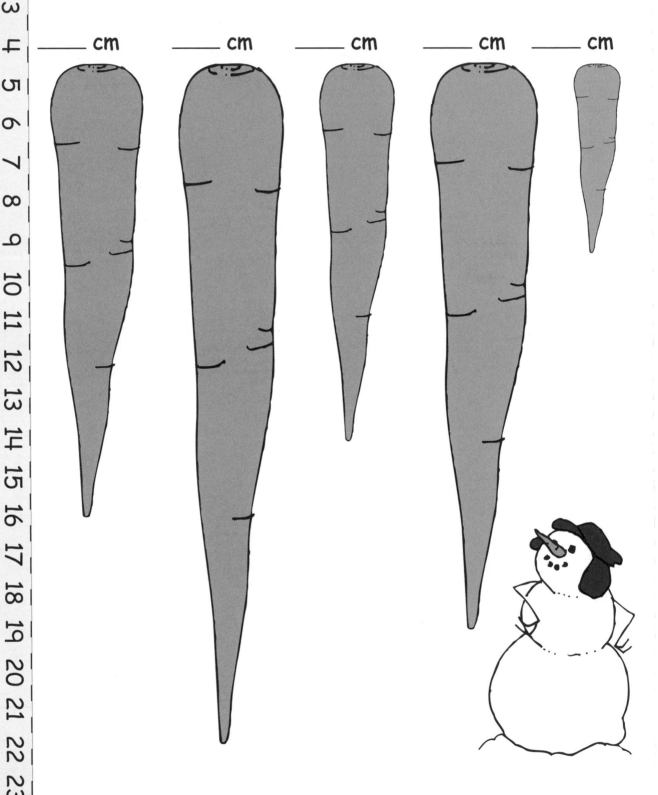

Skills: Measuring to the Nearest Centimeter

Math • EMC 4546 • ©2005 by Evan-Moor Corp.

Drip Drop

Draw lines to match the problems with their answers.

Skills:

Two-Digit
Addition with
Regrouping

73

$$\begin{array}{r} 26 \\ + 26 \\ \hline \end{array}$$

$$\begin{array}{r} 56 \\ + 35 \\ \hline \end{array}$$

87

$$\begin{array}{r} 28 \\ + 45 \\ \hline \end{array}$$

$$\begin{array}{r} 49 \\ + 38 \\ \hline \end{array}$$

52

96

91

$$\begin{array}{r} 54 \\ + 29 \\ \hline \end{array}$$

$$\begin{array}{r} 68 \\ + 28 \\ \hline \end{array}$$

65

$$\begin{array}{r} 19 \\ + 46 \\ \hline \end{array}$$

$$\begin{array}{r} 39 \\ + 39 \\ \hline \end{array}$$

44

78

$$\begin{array}{r} 15 \\ + 47 \\ \hline \end{array}$$

$$\begin{array}{r} 37 \\ + 7 \\ \hline \end{array}$$

62

83

Weather Watch

Graphing the Temperature

Weather Watch

This line graph shows the temperature for the first 18 days of July. Use the graph to answer the questions.

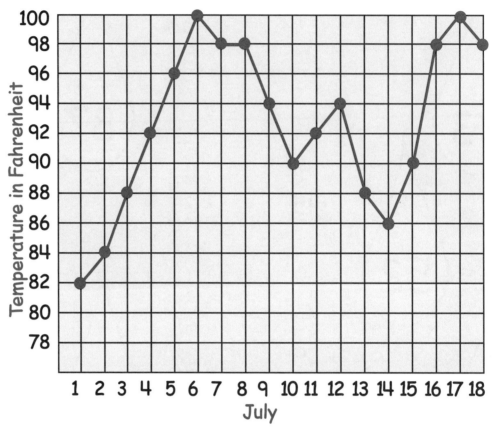

What was the temperature on the coldest day? _____

Which two days were the hottest? _____

How hot was it? _____

Starting with July 1, how many days
in a row did the temperature go up? _____

What was the temperature on July 10? _____

What was the difference between the
temperatures on July 14 and July 16? _____

What's the Temperature?

Skills:

Solving Word Problems

Write each problem. Then solve it.

The temperature this morning was 36 degrees. In the afternoon it was 27 degrees warmer. What was the afternoon temperature?

_____

In the afternoon the temperature was 65 degrees. In the evening it was 31 degrees cooler. What was the evening temperature?

_____

This morning the temperature was sixty-two degrees. Now it is nine degrees warmer. What is the temperature now?

_____

Dad says it may snow if the temperature falls to 32°F. It is 48° now. How many degrees must the temperature fall for it to snow?

_____

The hottest temperature of the year was 98°F. The coldest temperature of the year was 26°F. What was the difference between the hottest and the coldest temperatures?

_____

Mom says we cannot go swimming until the temperature reaches 75°. The thermometer now reads 60°. How much does the temperature need to rise before we can go swimming?

_____

Weather Watch

TEST YOUR SKILLS

Add or subtract.
Fill in the circle to show the answer.

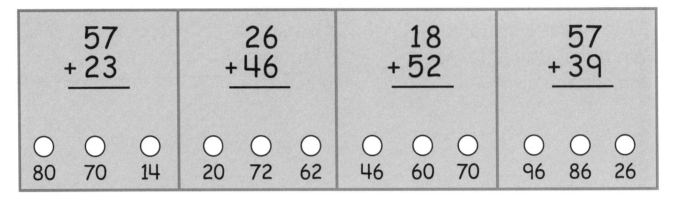

57 +23	26 +46	18 +52	57 +39
○ 80 ○ 70 ○ 14	○ 20 ○ 72 ○ 62	○ 46 ○ 60 ○ 70	○ 96 ○ 86 ○ 26

Write the temperature.

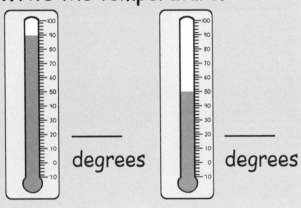

_____ degrees   _____ degrees

Color to show the fraction.

$\frac{2}{3}$ ○○○○○○

$\frac{1}{4}$

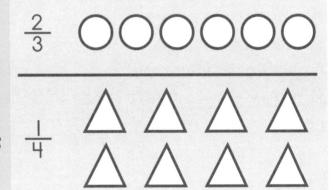

Count by 2s.

2   4   ☐   ☐   10   12   14   ☐   ☐   20   ☐   ☐

48 50 ☐   ☐   56   58   ☐   62   64   ☐   ☐   70

How long is it?

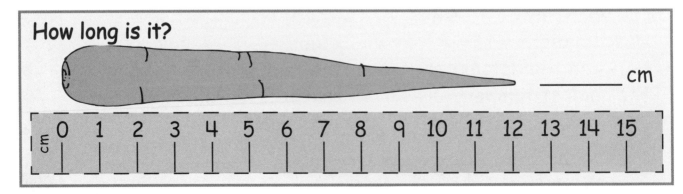

_____ cm

0 1 2 3 4 5 6 7 8 9 10 11 12 13 14 15

cm

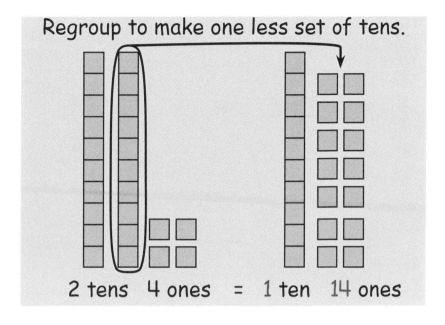

Regroup to make one less set of tens.

2 tens   4 ones   =   1 ten   14 ones

6 tens 5 ones = __5__ tens __15__ ones

9 tens 2 ones = __8__ tens __12__ ones

2 tens 7 ones = _____ tens _____ ones

8 tens 6 ones = _____ tens _____ ones

5 tens 8 ones = _____ tens _____ ones

6 tens 1 ones = _____ tens _____ ones

9 tens 4 ones = _____ tens _____ ones

7 tens 0 ones = _____ tens _____ ones

Outer Space

Up, Up, and Away!

Connect the dots. Start at **179**.

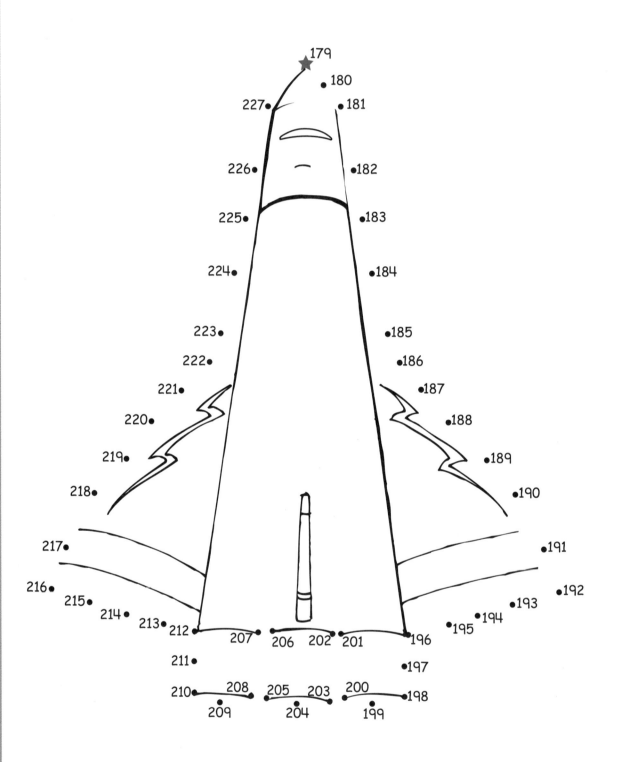

Outer Space

Skills:

Two-Digit Subtraction with Regrouping

Draw 2 tens sticks. Regroup a ten stick. Subtract 1 unit.

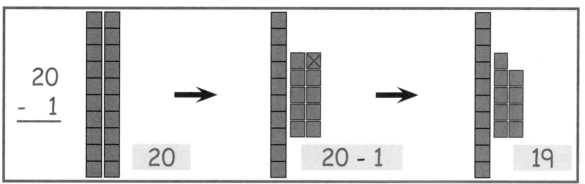

$$\begin{array}{r} 20 \\ -\ 1 \\ \hline \end{array}$$

20   20 - 1   19

Draw 2 tens sticks. Regroup a ten stick. Subtract 7 units.

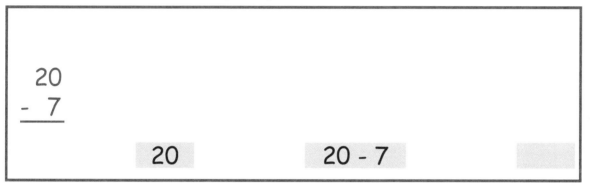

$$\begin{array}{r} 20 \\ -\ 7 \\ \hline \end{array}$$

20   20 - 7

Draw 3 tens sticks. Regroup a ten stick. Subtract 3 units.

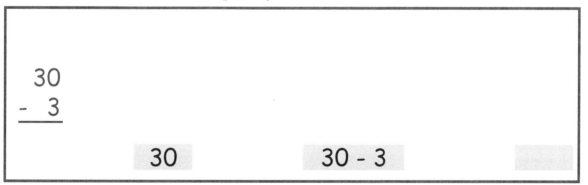

$$\begin{array}{r} 30 \\ -\ 3 \\ \hline \end{array}$$

30   30 - 3

Draw 3 tens sticks. Regroup a ten stick. Subtract 8 units.

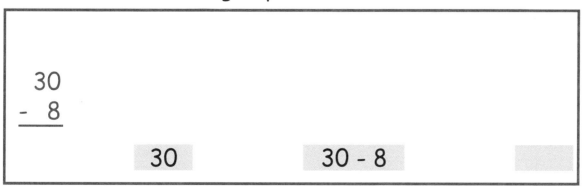

$$\begin{array}{r} 30 \\ -\ 8 \\ \hline \end{array}$$

30   30 - 8

Outer Space

Moon Craters

A scientific team set out to measure some moon craters. They measured the longest distance in meters.

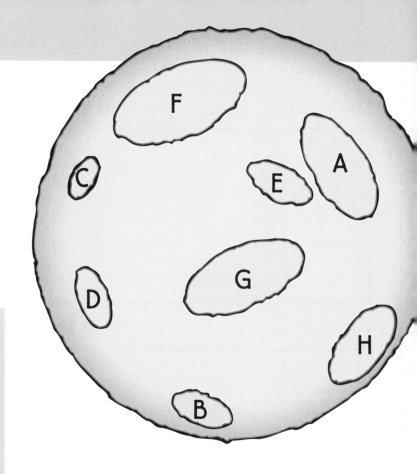

A 850 meters

B 532 meters

C 257 meters

D 300 meters

E 534 meters

F 983 meters

G 902 meters

H 775 meters

Which crater is the largest? ____

Which crater is the smallest? ____

Which craters are almost the same size? ____ ____

Which craters are longer than 780 meters? ____ ____ ____

Which crater measurement has **3** in the ones place? ____

Outer Space

Skills:

Two-Digit
Subtraction
with and
Without
Regrouping

Write the problems. Then solve them.

Rodney Rocketman is flying his ship through the asteroid belt. Yesterday he dodged 75 asteroids. Today he dodged only 47. How many more asteroids did he dodge yesterday?

_____

The space probe reached Jupiter 38 days after it was launched. It reached Neptune 95 days after it was launched. How many more days did it take to reach Neptune?

_____

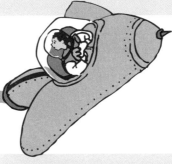

Uranus has 27 moons. Neptune has 13 moons. How many more moons does Uranus have?

_____

A year on Jupiter is about 12 Earth-years long. A year on Saturn is about 30 Earth-years long. How much longer is a year on Saturn?

_____

Outer Space

Subtraction with Regrouping

Skills:

Two-Digit
Subtraction with
Regrouping

This is what I think when I need to regroup to subtract:

I can't take 6 away from 4, so I must regroup the tens.

Now I have 2 tens and 14 ones.

$$14 - 6 = 8$$

2 tens - 0 tens = 2 tens

$$
\begin{array}{r}
\text{tens ones} \\
2\ 1 \\
\cancel{3}\cancel{4} \\
-\quad 6 \\
\hline
2\ 8
\end{array}
$$

$$
\begin{array}{r}
{}^{2}\cancel{3}{}^{1}0 \\
-\ \ 3 \\
\hline
27
\end{array}
\qquad
\begin{array}{r}
{}^{4}\cancel{5}{}^{1}1 \\
-\ \ 8 \\
\hline
\end{array}
\qquad
\begin{array}{r}
{}^{3}\cancel{4}{}^{1}3 \\
-\ \ 5 \\
\hline
\end{array}
\qquad
\begin{array}{r}
{}^{4}\cancel{5}{}^{1}0 \\
-\ \ 7 \\
\hline
\end{array}
\qquad
\begin{array}{r}
{}^{1}\cancel{2}{}^{1}8 \\
-\ \ 9 \\
\hline
\end{array}
$$

$$
\begin{array}{r}
74 \\
-\ 5 \\
\hline
\end{array}
\qquad
\begin{array}{r}
30 \\
-\ 1 \\
\hline
\end{array}
\qquad
\begin{array}{r}
34 \\
-\ 9 \\
\hline
\end{array}
\qquad
\begin{array}{r}
42 \\
-\ 3 \\
\hline
\end{array}
\qquad
\begin{array}{r}
23 \\
-\ 6 \\
\hline
\end{array}
$$

$$
\begin{array}{r}
21 \\
-\ 5 \\
\hline
\end{array}
\qquad
\begin{array}{r}
64 \\
-\ 9 \\
\hline
\end{array}
\qquad
\begin{array}{r}
55 \\
-\ 8 \\
\hline
\end{array}
\qquad
\begin{array}{r}
31 \\
-\ 5 \\
\hline
\end{array}
\qquad
\begin{array}{r}
77 \\
-\ 9 \\
\hline
\end{array}
$$

Skills:

Telling Time to
Five Minutes

The commander of Space Station Seven posted this list of chores to be done and the times by which they need to be finished.

Match the chore with the correct clock.

Station Chores

Service escape pods   2:15 •

Put fuel in shuttle   4:05 •

Clean video screen   7:45 •

Calibrate sensors   9:50 •

Program holodeck   6:10 •

Repair replicator   11:55 •

Outer Space

Riddle Time

If athletes get athlete's foot, what do astronauts get?

E – 39	L – 62	T – 47
G – 78	M – 36	Y – 24
H – 56	O – 89	
I – 17	S – 25	

$$\begin{array}{r} 91 \\ -\ 44 \\ \hline 47 \end{array} \qquad \begin{array}{r} 82 \\ -\ 26 \\ \hline \end{array} \qquad \begin{array}{r} 77 \\ -\ 38 \\ \hline \end{array} \qquad \begin{array}{r} 63 \\ -\ 39 \\ \hline \end{array}$$

I   ___   ___   ___

$$\begin{array}{r} 96 \\ -\ 18 \\ \hline \end{array} \qquad \begin{array}{r} 96 \\ -\ 57 \\ \hline \end{array} \qquad \begin{array}{r} 93 \\ -\ 46 \\ \hline \end{array}$$

___   ___   ___

$$\begin{array}{r} 95 \\ -\ 59 \\ \hline \end{array} \quad \begin{array}{r} 75 \\ -\ 58 \\ \hline \end{array} \quad \begin{array}{r} 50 \\ -\ 25 \\ \hline \end{array} \quad \begin{array}{r} 80 \\ -\ 55 \\ \hline \end{array} \quad \begin{array}{r} 80 \\ -\ 18 \\ \hline \end{array} \quad \begin{array}{r} 64 \\ -\ 25 \\ \hline \end{array}$$

___   ___   ___   ___   ___   ___

$$\begin{array}{r} 84 \\ -\ 37 \\ \hline \end{array} \qquad \begin{array}{r} 98 \\ -\ \ 9 \\ \hline \end{array} \qquad \begin{array}{r} 52 \\ -\ 13 \\ \hline \end{array}$$

___   ___   ___

How Many Moons?

Color the graph to show how many moons these planets have.

Mercury – no moons   Mars – 2 moons   Uranus – more than 18

Venus – no moons   Jupiter – more than 18   Neptune – 13 moons

Earth – 1 moon   Saturn – more than 18   Pluto – 1 moon

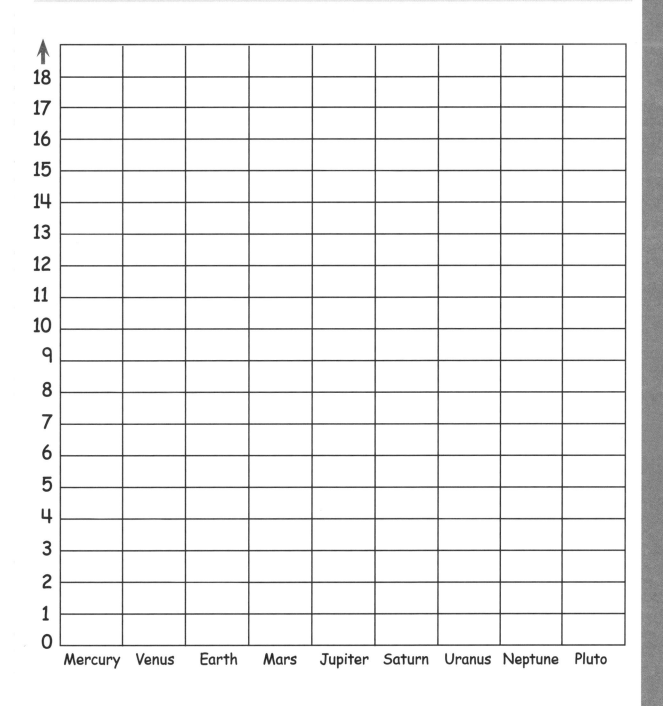

Outer Space

On the Moon

Write the problems. Then solve them.

The astronauts brought rocks back from the moon. The largest rock weighed 40 pounds. The smallest rock weighed 16 pounds. How much heavier was the largest rock?

pounds

Things weigh less on the moon than on Earth. If you weigh 54 pounds on Earth, you would weigh about 9 pounds on the moon. How much more do you weigh on Earth than on the moon?

pounds

There are many craters on the moon. One crater measured 95 yards across. Another crater measured 58 yards across. How much wider was the larger crater?

yards

You can leap much farther on the moon than on Earth. One astronaut leaped three times for a total of 63 feet. Another astronaut leaped twice and covered 49 feet. How much farther did the first astronaut leap?

feet

Outer Space

Math • EMC 4546 • ©2005 by Evan-Moor Corp.

Larger, Smaller, Before, After

Compare the numbers. Use **>** (greater than) or **<** (less than).

7 ◯ 8   0 ◯ 1   9 ◯ 8

34 ◯ 99   41 ◯ 40   77 ◯ 66

450 ◯ 449   305 ◯ 315   942 ◯ 952

700 ◯ 800   191 ◯ 189

Write the numbers that come before and after.

__28__ 29 __30__   ____ 88 ____

____ 243 ____   ____ 460 ____

____ 622 ____   ____ 806 ____

____ 60 ____   ____ 176 ____

____ 329 ____   ____ 519 ____

____ 781 ____   ____ 987 ____

Space Tic-Tac-Toe

Mark an **X** on problems where you had to regroup.
Mark an **O** on problems with no regrouping.

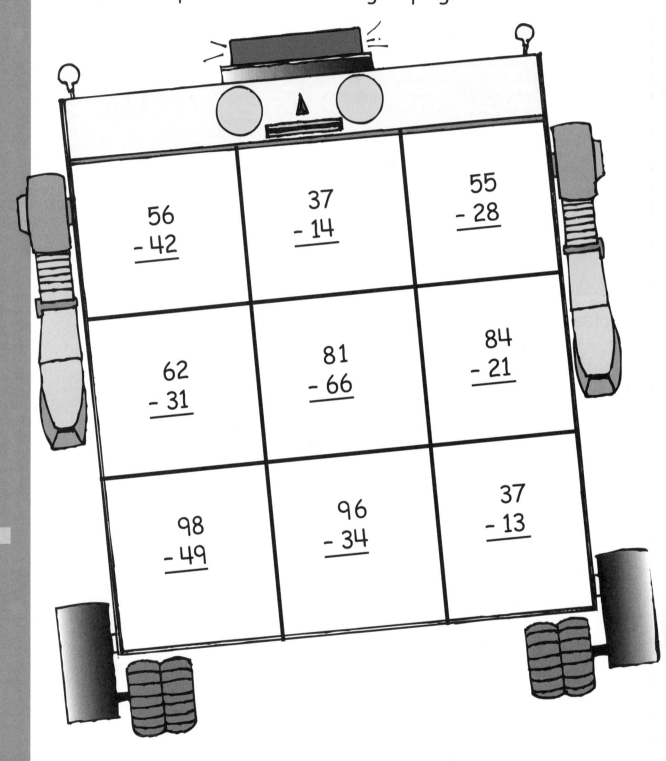

56 - 42	37 - 14	55 - 28
62 - 31	81 - 66	84 - 21
98 - 49	96 - 34	37 - 13

Who won? _____

TEST YOUR SKILLS

Add or subtract. You may or may not need to regroup.

15	12	34	86	42	41
+ 15	+ 29	− 16	− 16	+ 17	− 39

Read the thermometer.

Is it hot?　　○ Yes　　○ No

What is the temperature?

_____ degrees Fahrenheit

>, <, or = ?

450 ○ 350　　56 ○ 52　　111 ○ 113　　21 ○ 21

About how many centimeters?

_____

○ 2　　　　○ 10　　　　○ 30

Write the problem. Then solve it.

Toby Turtle finished the race in 77 seconds.
Teresa Turtle finished in 68 seconds.
How much slower was Toby?

_____ seconds slower

Celebration Times

Add.

Remember—if the ones are greater than 9, you must regroup and move the tens to the tens place.

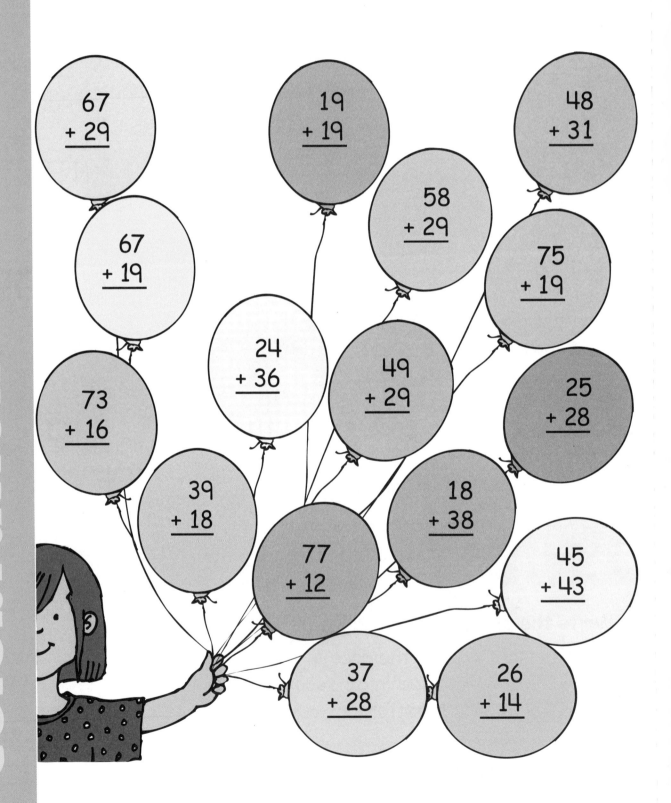

$$67 + 29$$

$$19 + 19$$

$$48 + 31$$

$$67 + 19$$

$$58 + 29$$

$$75 + 19$$

$$24 + 36$$

$$49 + 29$$

$$25 + 28$$

$$73 + 16$$

$$39 + 18$$

$$18 + 38$$

$$45 + 43$$

$$77 + 12$$

$$37 + 28$$

$$26 + 14$$

Math • EMC 4546 • ©2005 by Evan-Moor Corp.

The distance around something is called the perimeter.
How far is it around each shape?

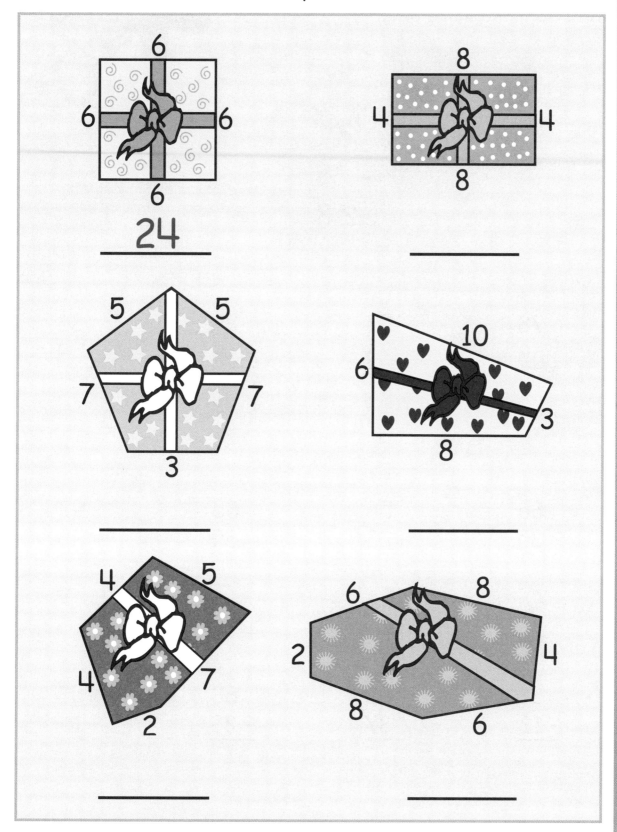

Celebration Times

Ring in the New!

Skills:

Two-Digit
Subtraction
with and
Without
Regrouping

Subtract. Remember, if there are not enough ones to subtract, regroup the tens to make more ones.

```
  tens ones
   2  1
   3  1
 -    3
 ───────
   2  8
```

78	57	29	36
- 9	- 26	- 4	- 9

66	56	85	47
- 35	- 28	- 65	- 25

22	93	68	52
- 12	- 37	- 29	- 16

Math • EMC 4546 • ©2005 by Evan-Moor Corp.

You're Having a Party!

Here are the prices of some items you might want to have at your party. Use the information to help you write and solve each problem.

balloon	party favor	party hat	noisemaker
$1.00 each	$5.00 each	$2.00 each	$3.00 each

1 How much will it cost for each person if you buy all of the party items shown?

_____

3 You've decided to have only balloons and party hats. How many friends can you invite if you have $15.00 to spend?

_____

2 You have $30.00 to spend. Can you buy all of the items for three guests?

_____

4 This is what you bought:

5

10

5 🎁

How much did you spend?

_____

©2005 by Evan-Moor Corp. • EMC 4546 • Math

Celebration Times

Here Comes the Parade

We saw these things in the parade:

7 bands	**12** clowns
4 dogs	**10** floats
11 funny cars	**9** bicycles
5 balloons	**8** horses
3 fire trucks	

Label the graph and color in the sections to show the information above.

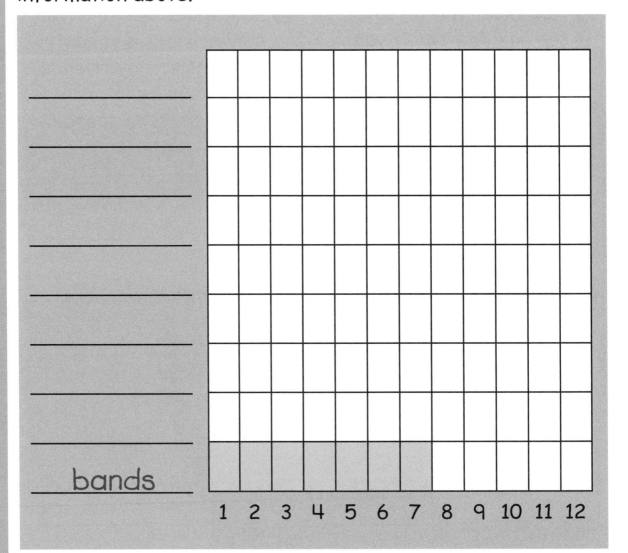

bands

1 2 3 4 5 6 7 8 9 10 11 12

Math • EMC 4546 • ©2005 by Evan-Moor Corp.

Skills:

Two-Digit Addition with and Without Regrouping

I may promise you a treasure, but watch out! I'm tricky.

P	N	E
21 + 46	56 + 43	17 + 29

R	L	C
55 + 14	39 + 16	45 + 25

E	A	U
28 + 18	48 + 28	28 + 53

H	A
67 + 26	39 + 37

Write the letter that goes with each answer.

___ ___ ___ ___ ___ ___ ___ ___ ___ ___ ___
76   55 46 67 69 46 70 93 76 81 99

©2005 by Evan-Moor Corp. • EMC 4546 • Math

Celebration Times

The Clowns Go Marching

Skills:

Ordinal Numbers
Patterning

Write the correct ordinal number under each clown.

fourth	second	sixth
third	fifth	first

Each clown had an umbrella. Label the pattern.

A __ __ __ __ __ __ __

Math • EMC 4546 • ©2005 by Evan-Moor Corp.

Skills:

Two-Digit Subtraction with and Without Regrouping

What do you always get a new one of, even if the old one was good?

A - 47	N - 23	W - 15
E - 56	R - 38	Y - 22

```
  67          90      82      73
- 20        - 67    - 26    - 58
```
☐ ☐ ☐ ☐

___ ___ ___ ___

```
  90      94      58      76
- 68    - 38    - 11    - 38
```
☐ ☐ ☐ ☐

___ ___ ___ ___

Celebration Times

Symmetrical Symbols

When you draw a line of symmetry, both sides are the same. Are both sides the same?

Draw a line of symmetry on each symbol.

Celebration Times

Skills:

Two-Digit Addition and Subtraction with and Without Regrouping

Be careful. Some problems require regrouping; some do not.

When you are finished, color the squares with problems where you did not regroup.

23 + 46	75 + 19	71 + 28	37 + 28	65 − 34
48 − 26	89 − 25	99 − 63	43 − 27	33 + 66
57 − 14	94 − 66	54 + 35	66 − 47	78 − 30

Celebration Times

What is the secret message? _____

Hidden Holiday Picture

A line that connects two points is called a line segment.
We write line segments like this: $\overline{XY}$

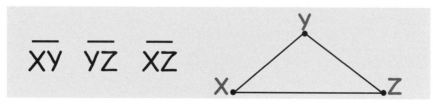

$$\overline{XY} \quad \overline{YZ} \quad \overline{XZ}$$

Draw these line segments to see what's hiding.

$$\overline{AB} \quad \overline{BG} \quad \overline{GH} \quad \overline{HA} \quad \overline{BC} \quad \overline{GF} \quad \overline{CF} \quad \overline{CD} \quad \overline{DE} \quad \overline{EF}$$

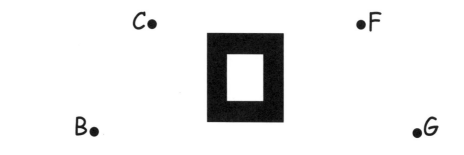

D•

•E

C•

•F

B•

G•

A•

•H

The picture you made might belong to

88

UNIT 7

Math • EMC 4546 • ©2005 by Evan-Moor Corp.

TEST YOUR SKILLS

Subtract.

78	45	56	93
- 29	- 27	- 28	- 37

◯ ◯ ◯ ◯ ◯ ◯ ◯ ◯ ◯ ◯ ◯ ◯
48 97 49   22 18 72   28 34 84   68 64 56

Draw a line of symmetry.

How far is it around each shape?
Fill in the circle to show the answer.

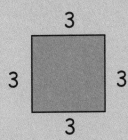

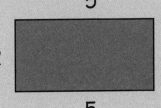

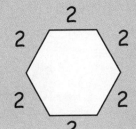

◯ ◯ ◯   ◯ ◯ ◯   ◯ ◯ ◯
15 9 12   12 14 16   12 14 20

Write the correct ordinal number under each clown.

| third |
| first |
| fourth |
| second |

Label the pattern.

____ ____ ____ ____ ____ ____ ____ ____ ____

How Many Legs?

Skills:

Concept of Multiplication

How many dogs?	2
How many legs on each dog?	4
How many legs in all?	8

How many birds? _____

How many legs on each bird? _____

How many legs in all? _____

How many insects? _____

How many legs on each insect? _____

How many legs in all? _____

How many horses? _____

How many legs on each horse? _____

How many legs in all? _____

How many birds? _____

How many legs on each bird? _____

How many legs in all? _____

Animals, Animals

Math • EMC 4546 • ©2005 by Evan-Moor Corp.

Write each problem. Then solve it.

Timothy Turtle's favorite food is cabbage leaves. He ate 3 leaves from each of 3 cabbage plants. How many leaves did Timothy eat?

_____ leaves

Timothy is slow, but steady. He walked 1 mile every day for 5 days to get to the cabbage patch. How many miles did Timothy walk?

_____ miles

Timothy's shell has square shapes on it. There are 5 rows of squares. Each row has 5 squares. How many squares are on Timothy's shell?

_____ squares

Timothy pulls his head and legs inside his shell when he takes a nap. Timothy took 2 naps each day on Monday, Tuesday, and Wednesday. How many naps did he take?

_____ naps

Timothy joined 3 other turtles at the pond to catch flies. Each turtle caught 4 flies. How many flies were eaten in all?

_____ flies

Animals, Animals

Home to the Hive

Connect the flowers to help Buzz Bee find his way back to the hive. You must always move to a larger number and in order.

Animals, Animals

UNIT 8

Math • EMC 4546 • ©2005 by Evan-Moor Corp.

How Many Spots?

__3__ dogs x __2__ spots each = __6__ spots in all

_____ dogs x _____ spots each = _____ spots in all

_____ dogs x _____ spots each = _____ spots in all

_____ dogs x _____ spots each = _____ spots in all

Animals, Animals

At the Roundup

Rancher Ron wants to round up some of the cattle in each herd. Color the fractions shown.

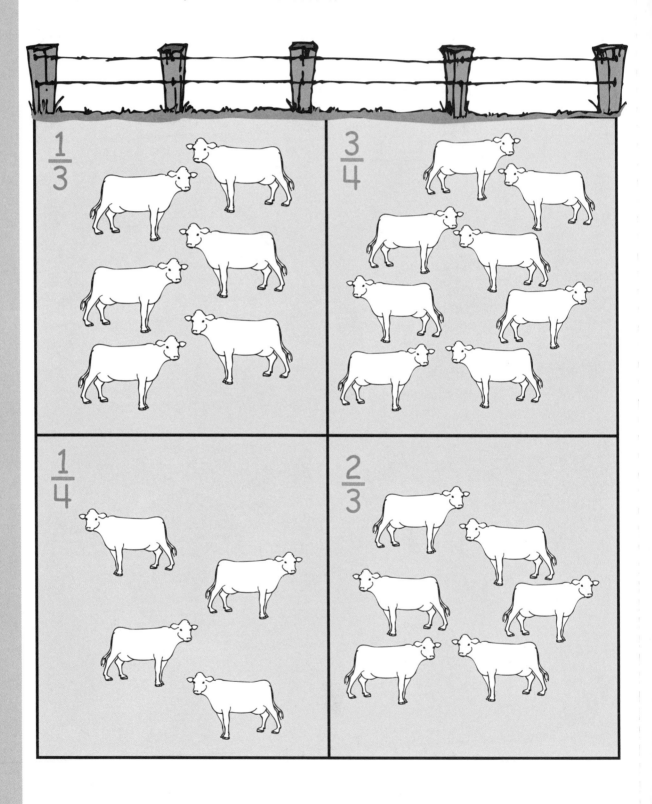

Counting Elephants

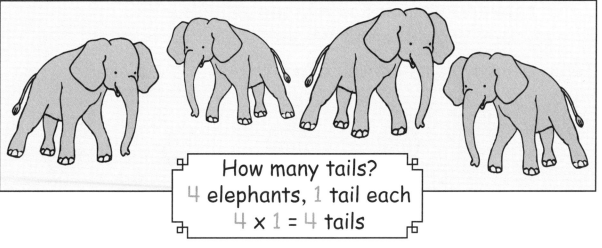

How many tails?
4 elephants, 1 tail each
4 x 1 = 4 tails

How many ears?

_____ elephants, _____ ears each

_____ x _____ = _____ ears

How many legs?

_____ elephants, _____ legs each

_____ x _____ = _____ legs

How many tusks?

_____ elephants, _____ tusks each

_____ x _____ = _____ tusks

How many trunks?

_____ elephants, _____ trunks each

_____ x _____ = _____ trunks

Animals, Animals

Sticker Fun

Robert collects stickers of African animals.
The stickers are different prices.

Tell how many coins he would use to buy each sticker.

15¢		1	1	
20¢				
32¢				
28¢				
50¢				
43¢				
65¢				
39¢				

Math • EMC 4546 • ©2005 by Evan-Moor Corp.

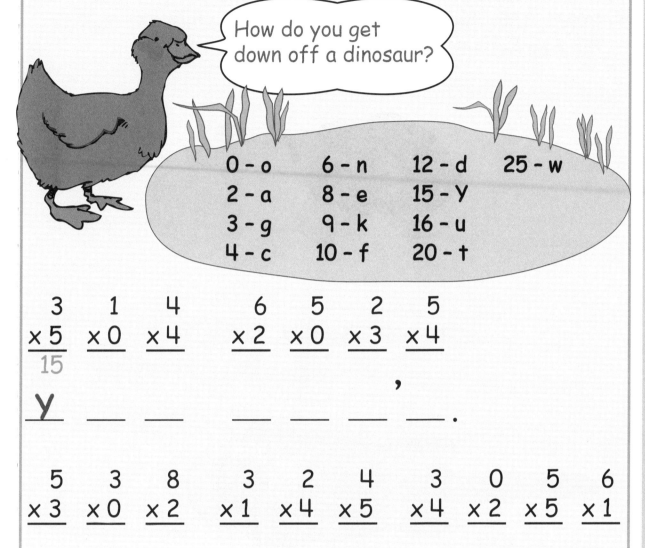

How do you get
down off a dinosaur?

0 – o	6 – n	12 – d	25 – w
2 – a	8 – e	15 – Y	
3 – g	9 – k	16 – u	
4 – c	10 – f	20 – t	

$$\begin{array}{c}3\\ \times 5\\ \hline 15\end{array} \quad \begin{array}{c}1\\ \times 0\\ \hline\end{array} \quad \begin{array}{c}4\\ \times 4\\ \hline\end{array} \quad \begin{array}{c}6\\ \times 2\\ \hline\end{array} \quad \begin{array}{c}5\\ \times 0\\ \hline\end{array} \quad \begin{array}{c}2\\ \times 3\\ \hline\end{array} \quad \begin{array}{c}5\\ \times 4\\ \hline\end{array}$$

,

Y __ __ __ __ __ __ — .

$$\begin{array}{c}5\\ \times 3\\ \hline\end{array} \quad \begin{array}{c}3\\ \times 0\\ \hline\end{array} \quad \begin{array}{c}8\\ \times 2\\ \hline\end{array} \quad \begin{array}{c}3\\ \times 1\\ \hline\end{array} \quad \begin{array}{c}2\\ \times 4\\ \hline\end{array} \quad \begin{array}{c}4\\ \times 5\\ \hline\end{array} \quad \begin{array}{c}3\\ \times 4\\ \hline\end{array} \quad \begin{array}{c}0\\ \times 2\\ \hline\end{array} \quad \begin{array}{c}5\\ \times 5\\ \hline\end{array} \quad \begin{array}{c}6\\ \times 1\\ \hline\end{array}$$

__ __ __ __ __ __ __ __ __ __

$$\begin{array}{c}0\\ \times 4\\ \hline\end{array} \quad \begin{array}{c}2\\ \times 5\\ \hline\end{array} \quad \begin{array}{c}5\\ \times 2\\ \hline\end{array} \quad\quad \begin{array}{c}1\\ \times 2\\ \hline\end{array} \quad\quad \begin{array}{c}4\\ \times 3\\ \hline\end{array} \quad \begin{array}{c}4\\ \times 4\\ \hline\end{array} \quad \begin{array}{c}2\\ \times 2\\ \hline\end{array} \quad \begin{array}{c}3\\ \times 3\\ \hline\end{array}$$

__ __ __ __ __ __ __ __ __ !

Put Them on the Shelf

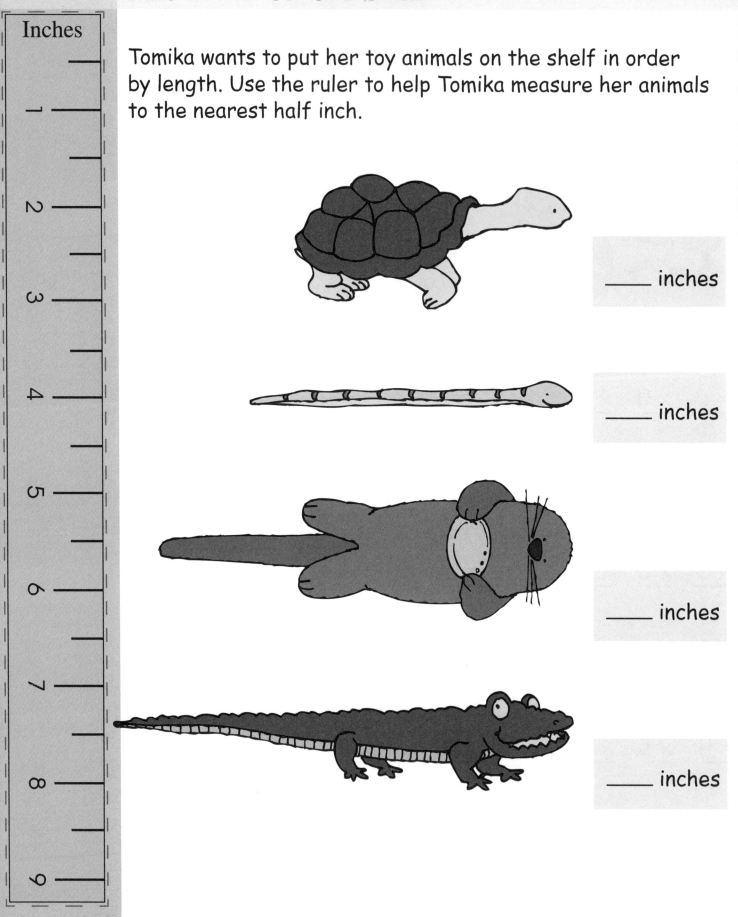

Tomika wants to put her toy animals on the shelf in order by length. Use the ruler to help Tomika measure her animals to the nearest half inch.

_____ inches

_____ inches

_____ inches

_____ inches

Inches

1
2
3
4
5
6
7
8
9

Skills: Measuring to the Nearest Half Inch

Math • EMC 4546 • ©2005 by Evan-Moor Corp.

Write each problem. Then solve it.

Farmer Dave has 6 hens. Each hen lays one egg a day. How many eggs will Farmer Dave collect in 3 days?

_____ eggs

The chickens sleep in cubes stacked together. There are 3 rows with 4 cubes in each row. How many chickens can take a rest at one time?

_____ chickens

Each chick eats 2 pounds of feed every week. How much feed will 8 chicks eat in a week?

_____ pounds of feed

Sometimes Farmer Dave lets the eggs hatch. Last month 3 hens hatched 5 eggs each. How many new chicks are in the coop?

_____ chicks

On Monday Farmer Dave sold 4 eggs to his neighbor. The neighbor wanted to bake a cake. She paid 5¢ an egg. How much money was Farmer Dave paid?

_____ ¢

Animals, Animals

Animal Tracks

Color each set of animal tracks to show the pattern written.

ABCC

AAB

ABAC

Animals, Animals

Help the Cows Get Home

Solve the problems. Color the answers in order to show the cows how to get home.

2	4	3	5	6	4	5	2
x 3	x 2	x 3	x 1	x 0	x 3	x 5	x 2
6							

2	5	5	6	8	4	9	0
x 1	x 2	x 3	x 3	x 2	x 5	x 2	x 4

6	2	6	20	25	16
8	5	12	4	0	9
9	5	0	12	25	6
8	4	15	9	4	3
6	12	15	10	2	8
9	16	18	12	4	10
0	2	16	20	18	0

Animals, Animals

TEST YOUR SKILLS

Add or subtract.

75	46	316	95	68	47
− 27	+ 29	+ 183	− 43	− 19	+ 37

Fill in the blanks.

_____ groups of _____

_____ × _____ = _____

_____ groups of _____

_____ × _____ = _____

Multiply.

4 × 3 = _____   6 × 2 = _____   5 × 5 = _____   1 × 3 = _____

What is the perimeter?

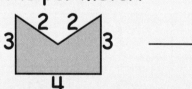   _____

Draw lines of symmetry.

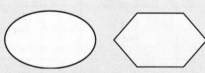

Color ⅓.

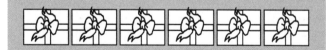

Mark 63¢.

Draw a line 4½ inches long.

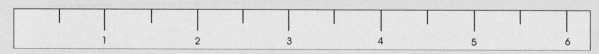

    Math • EMC 4546 • ©2005 by Evan-Moor Corp.

Skills:

Multiplication
Facts

Write multiplication problems to show how many flowers.
Then solve each problem.

_____ x _____ = _____

_____ x _____ = _____

_____ x _____ = _____

_____ x _____ = _____

In the Garden

Skills:

Two- and Three-Digit Addition & Subtraction with and Without Regrouping

Column Addition

59 + 24	72 + 16	43 + 46	73 + 55	46 + 44	60 + 39

36 − 14	53 − 14	99 − 11	41 − 29	62 − 33	50 − 25

222 − 200	432 + 135	612 + 243	668 − 240	790 − 190	576 − 251

5 4 4 6 2 + 8	2 2 2 2 2 + 2	5 5 5 5 5 + 5	1 9 8 2 2 + 8	6 4 7 3 8 + 2	2 3 4 5 2 + 1

In the Garden

104   **UNIT 9**

Math • EMC 4546 • ©2005 by Evan-Moor Corp.

Farmer Smith's Rain Gauges

It is important for Farmer Smith to know how much rain his crops are getting. He measures every rainfall.

Here are his rain records for 7 days. The gauges show rainfall in inches.

Make a graph to show the information.

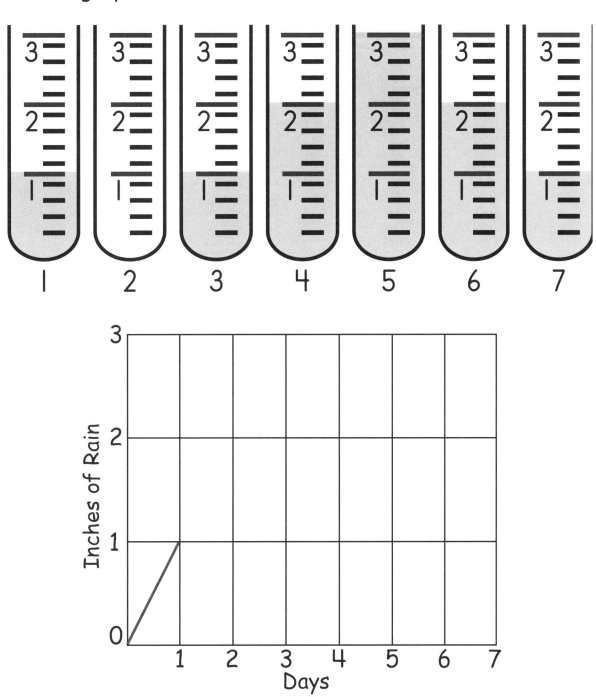

In the Garden

A Garden Riddle

You throw away the outside and cook the inside. Then you eat the outside and throw away the inside. What is it?

A – 12	E – 0	N – 6	R – 4
C – 16	F – 9	O – 18	

```
  6       2              5       4       2
 x2      x3             x0      x3      x2
[___]   [___]          [___]   [___]   [___]

___     ___            ___     ___     ___
```

```
  9       3              4       6       1       1
 x2      x3             x4      x3      x4      x6
[___]   [___]          [___]   [___]   [___]   [___]

___     ___            ___     ___     ___     ___
```

In the Garden

Skills:

Solving Word
Problems

Write each problem. Then solve it.

Elisa is planting bulbs. She bought 5 bags of tulip bulbs. There are 5 bulbs in each bag. How many bulbs will she plant?

_____ bulbs

Jamal wants to plant 25 daffodils. He bought 6 bags, each with 4 bulbs. Does he have the number he wants to plant?

_____

Ian wants to plant irises. Irises are sold in bags of 3. He bought 4 bags. How many irises will Ian plant?

_____ irises

There are ten bags of crocuses on the shelf. Each bag holds 10 bulbs. How many crocus bulbs are there?

_____ crocus bulbs

Jennifer is planting paper whites. She dug 10 holes. She has 6 bags with 2 bulbs in each bag. How many more holes must she dig?

_____ holes

In the Garden

Picking for Pennies

Penny's mom has a garden. Penny earns money picking fruits and vegetables. Here is yesterday's harvest.

Complete the table to show what Penny earned yesterday.

Crop	Amount Picked	Amount Paid for Each	Amount Earned
Strawberries		2¢	
Tomatoes		3¢	
Pumpkins		5¢	
Corn		4¢	
Beans		1¢	

How much did Penny earn in all? _____

Math • EMC 4546 • ©2005 by Evan-Moor Corp.

Paste each problem in the seed packet where it belongs.

8 × 2

6 × 2

4 × 4

4 × 3

4 × 5

4 × 2

8 × 1

10 × 2

paste

paste

paste

paste

paste

paste

paste

paste

In the Garden

Skills: Multiplication Facts

Harvest Time

Solve the problems to see how many of each vegetable
Farmer Fred harvested.

$$\begin{array}{r} 6 \\ \times\,2 \\ \hline \end{array}$$

$$\begin{array}{r} 3 \\ \times\,3 \\ \hline \end{array}$$

$$\begin{array}{r} 4 \\ \times\,2 \\ \hline \end{array}$$

$1 \times 4 =$ _____

$3 \times 4 =$ _____

$5 \times 5 =$ _____

$2 \times 0 =$ _____

$5 \times 3 =$ _____

$2 \times 3 =$ _____

How many green vegetables? _____

How many red vegetables? _____

How many yellow vegetables? _____

How many orange vegetables? _____

In the Garden

Math • EMC 4546 • ©2005 by Evan-Moor Corp.

Skills:

Telling Time
to the Nearest
Half-hour

Roberto keeps track of the time each of his garden chores takes.

Here is his record for last Saturday. How much time did he spend on each task?

Weeding

| Start | Stop | How much time? |

 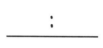

_____ : _____

Watering

| Start | Stop | How much time? |

_____ : _____

Planting and Pruning

| Start | Stop | How much time? |

_____ : _____

Picking Ripe Fruits and Vegetables

| Start | Stop | How much time? |

_____ : _____

★Super Bonus: How much time did Roberto spend in the garden last Saturday? _____

In the Garden

How Does Your Garden Grow?

Write each problem. Then solve it.

Don wants to plant 24 carrot plants. He has planted 15. How many more carrots does he need to plant?

_____ carrots

Jan planted 150 lettuce plants on Saturday. She has 126 left to plant on Sunday. How many plants will she have planted in all?

_____ plants

Ron picked 21 cucumbers one day and 29 cucumbers a week later. How many cucumbers has he picked?

_____ cucumbers

Fred has 4 baskets of strawberries. There are 10 berries in each basket. How many berries are there in all?

_____ berries

Shelley made a fruit basket for a friend. The basket held four oranges, six apples, five bananas, and five pears. How much fruit was in the basket?

_____ pieces of fruit

In the Garden

Math • EMC 4546 • ©2005 by Evan-Moor Corp.

Gardening Patterns

All gardeners have a way they like to plant the rows in their gardens. Look at each gardener's pattern and label it.

____ ____ ____ ____ ____ ____

____ ____ ____ ____ ____ ____ ____ ____ ____ ____

____ ____ ____ ____ ____ ____ ____ ____

How would you plant your garden?
Draw and label your pattern.

TEST YOUR SKILLS

Write the multiplication problem to show how many apples.

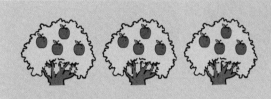

_____ X _____ = _____   _____ X _____ = _____

Add or subtract.

59	62	612	576	438
− 24	− 33	+ 243	− 251	+ 250

Read the problem. Write the answer.

Betty picked 3 baskets of apples. There are 9 apples in each basket. How many apples did she pick in all?

_____ apples

Read the clocks.

How much time passed?

_____ : _____

Multiply. Fill in the circle to show the answer.

6 x 2 =	3 x 4 =	5 x 5 =	2 x 8 =
○ ○ ○	○ ○ ○	○ ○ ○	○ ○ ○
8 10 12	14 12 7	25 15 10	30 10 16

Math • EMC 4546 • ©2005 by Evan-Moor Corp.

Skills:

Addition and Subtraction Facts to 18

Column Addition

You have reached the last unit in this book. It will review most of the math skills you did in Units 1-9. At the end of Unit 10 is a 2-page Test Your Skills that will help you see how well you know the math skills in this book. Good luck!

9 + 9	5 + 8	13 - 4	8 + 4	14 - 5	18 - 9

16 - 8	8 + 7	14 - 6	7 + 6	9 + 6	15 - 9

13 - 6	12 - 3	9 + 4	7 + 9	9 + 5	15 - 6

16 - 7	13 - 5	17 - 8	8 - 8	4 + 9	12 - 8

9 5 + 1	8 4 + 2	7 7 + 4	9 8 + 0	4 9 + 4	6 3 + 4

The Beautiful Sea

Beach Geometry

Skills:

Perimeter
Symmetry

What is the perimeter of each figure?

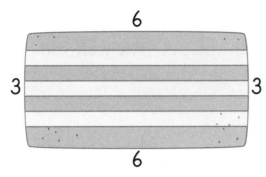

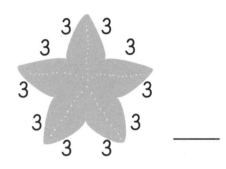

_____

_____

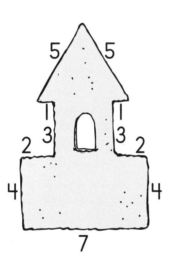

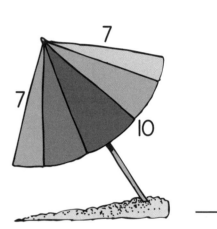

_____

_____

Are the two parts of each figure symmetrical?

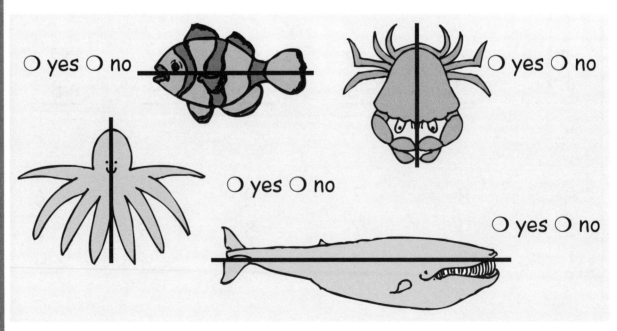

○ yes ○ no

○ yes ○ no

○ yes ○ no

○ yes ○ no

Math • EMC 4546 • ©2005 by Evan-Moor Corp.

The Beautiful Sea

Skills:

Solving Word Problems

Write each problem. Then solve it.

Bo and Jo were collecting shells at the beach. Bo took home 23 shells. Jo took home 29 shells. How many shells did they collect together?

_____ shells

We counted mussels on 8 rocks in the tide pool. There were 3 mussels on each rock. How many mussels were there?

_____ mussels

We saw 34 crabs scurrying along the beach. A big wave took 16 crabs out to sea. How many crabs were left on the beach?

_____ crabs

The octopus ate 4 crabs each day for 5 days. How many crabs did the octopus eat?

_____ crabs

I counted the floats on four strands of seaweed. Here is my count: 5 floats, 7 floats, 4 floats, 3 floats. How many floats in all?

_____ floats

My seashell collection is too big. I gave my friend Rod 27 of my 75 shells. How many shells are left in my collection?

_____ shells

The Beautiful Sea

Measurement Review

A bat ray measures 30 inches across. About how many centimeters would it measure?

○ 30   ○ 25   ○ 15   ○ 75

I measured the height of my sand castle in both inches and centimeters. Which measurement would show the larger number of units?

○ inches   ○ centimeters

A sea snail crawled 24 inches in 15 minutes. About how far would that be in centimeters?

○ 30   ○ 60   ○ 25   ○ 40

A shell is 5 centimeters long. About how many inches is that? (Look at the rulers below.) About _____ inches.

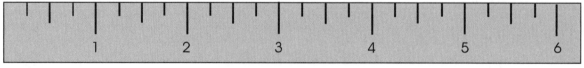

Inches

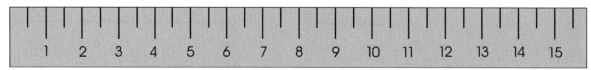

Centimeters

The Beautiful Sea

Two-Digit Addition and Subtraction

Skills:

Two-Digit Addition and Subtraction with and Without Regrouping

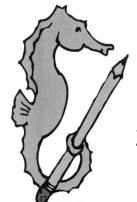

20	19	55	10	29
+ 60	+ 22	+ 35	+ 81	+ 39

38	44	32	43	97	45
− 21	− 32	− 13	− 27	− 19	− 26

72	66	52	66	43	55
− 27	+ 26	+ 47	− 22	− 29	− 49

77	76	38	30	33	80
− 27	+ 18	+ 27	− 11	− 25	− 11

68	71	50	37	45	29
− 21	+ 19	− 34	+ 37	+ 24	− 10

The Beautiful Sea

Order and Patterns

This school of fish will help you review numbers and patterns.

Write to tell the order.

second   fifth   first   third   fourth

_____

_____

_____

_____

_____

What is the pattern?

_____

Color these fish to show the pattern ABCBC.

Math • EMC 4546 • ©2005 by Evan-Moor Corp.

The Beautiful Sea

Skills:

Two-Digit Addition and Subtraction with and Without Regrouping

I'm a strange-looking shark. In fact, my head looks like a tool used to build things. What is my name?

| A – 85 | D – 92 | E – 76 | H – 46 |
| K – 59 | M – 27 | R – 38 | S – 63 |

94
– 48

49
+ 36

76
– 49

64
– 37

48
+ 28

84
– 46

82
– 36

37
+ 39

47
+ 38

64
+ 28

25
+ 38

63
– 17

26
+ 59

90
– 52

92
– 33

Which one do I look like?

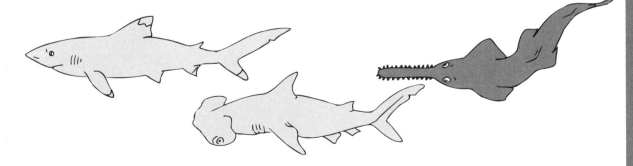

The Beautiful Sea

Money and Time

Skills:

Value of Coins
Making Change
Telling Time to
Five Minutes

The Beautiful Sea

Cost	Give Clerk	How Much Change?

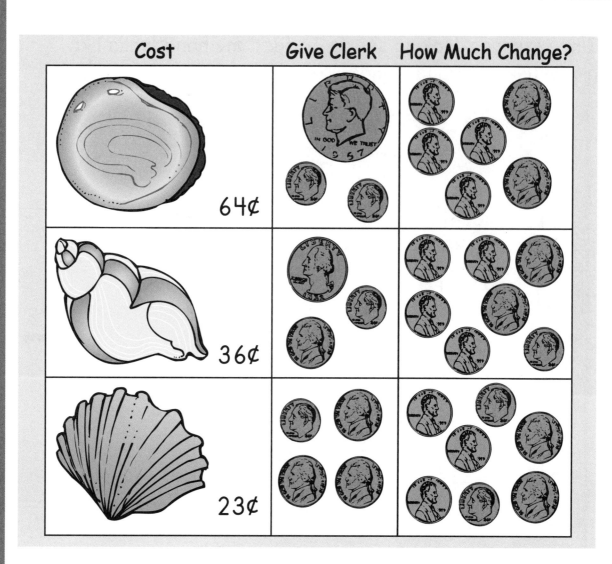

64¢

36¢

23¢

Match.

1:25 •

8:30 •

10:45 •

2:15 •

Three-Digit Addition and Subtraction

Skills:

Three-Digit
Addition and
Subtraction
Without
Regrouping

```
  689        655        735
- 465      - 324      - 123
```

```
  252        405        721
+ 346      + 550      +  75
```

```
  488      958       777       105        263
- 408    - 427     - 453     + 382      + 336
```

```
  500       687       153       692        200
+ 326     - 445     + 443     - 290      + 199
```

The Beautiful Sea

Knowing Numbers

Skills:

Place Value
Counting by 2s
Number Order

Circle the tens. Box the ones.

52	85
17	92
48	37

Before and After

_____, 100, 101

52, _____, 54

88, 89, _____

Connect the dots. Count by 2s.

UNIT 10

The Beautiful Sea

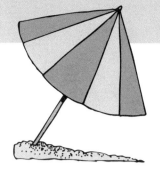

3 x 4 = _____   2 x 2 = _____   3 x 2 = _____

5 x 2 = _____   1 x 3 = _____   4 x 3 = _____

6 x 3 = _____   2 x 4 = _____   5 x 4 = _____

8	4	9	7	3	7
x 2	x 4	x 2	x 0	x 5	x 3

6	1	3	4	8	5
x 4	x 5	x 3	x 2	x 3	x 0

5	6	4	3	3	5
x 5	x 2	x 5	x 1	x 6	x 3

The Beautiful Sea

Fishy Fractions

Color the fractional amount of each school of fish.

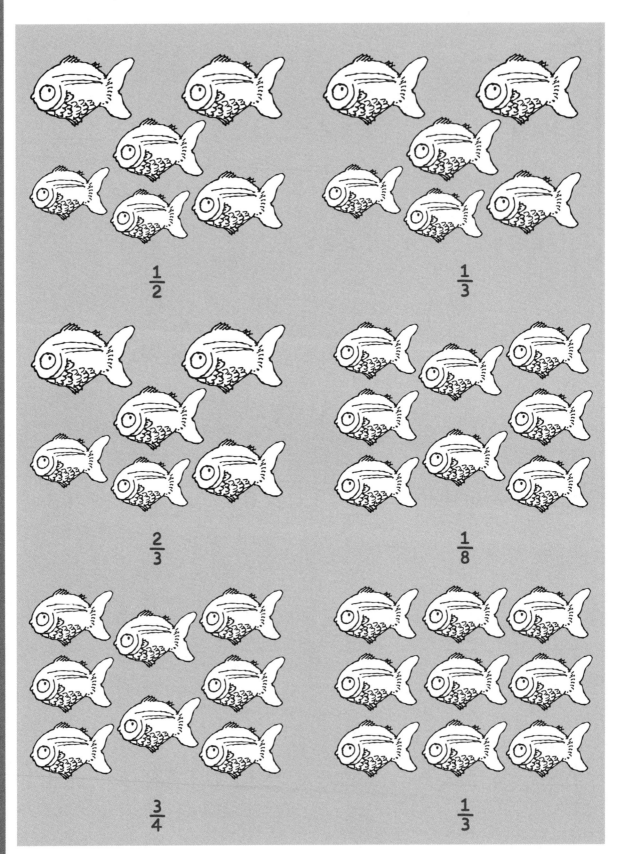

$\frac{1}{2}$

$\frac{1}{3}$

$\frac{2}{3}$

$\frac{1}{8}$

$\frac{3}{4}$

$\frac{1}{3}$

126

Math • EMC 4546 • ©2005 by Evan-Moor Corp.

Skills:

Geometric Shapes

Fractions of a Set

The Beautiful Sea

TEST YOUR SKILLS

Match.

seventy-two•   •400

four hundred•   •96

ninety-six•   •72

Before and After

____ 100 ____

____ 69 ____

____ 750 ____

>, <, or = ?

75 ◯ 92

4 + 5 ◯ 14 - 5

157 ◯ 155

Add or subtract.

$$452 + 347$$

$$95 - 49$$

$$361 + 438$$

$$57 + 18$$

$$48 + 38$$

$$82 - 47$$

Multiply.

5 x 3 = ____   3 x 0 = ____   6 x 2 = ____   1 x 4 = ____

$$7 \times 2$$

$$5 \times 5$$

$$4 \times 2$$

$$2 \times 1$$

$$2 \times 2$$

$$3 \times 3$$

Continue the pattern. Label it.

_____

Write the fraction.

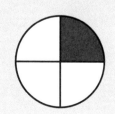

_____

Color the fraction. $\frac{1}{2}$

©2005 by Evan-Moor Corp. • EMC 4546 • Math   **ASSESSMENT 10**   **127**

TEST YOUR SKILLS

What time is it?

_____ : _____   _____ : _____

Match.

square •

cube •

rectangle •

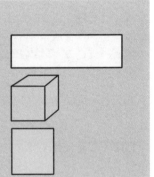

Measure.

_____ ____ inches

_____ ____ centimeters

Draw 2 lines of symmetry.

Find the perimeter.

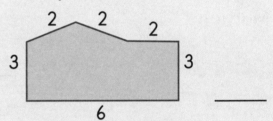

2   2   2

3   3

6

____

Make a graph.

Team	Games Won
Tigers	8
Bears	4
Lions	6
Bobcats	7

_____

_____

_____

_____

Write the problem. Then solve it.

Brian divided his animal stamps into piles of 5. He had 5 piles. How many animal stamps did Brian have?

____ animal stamps

Tracking Form

Topic	Color in each page you complete.						
Field Day Fun	3	4	5	6	7	8	9
	10	11	12	13	14		
At the Market	15	16	17	18	19	20	21
	22	23	24	25	26	27	
In the Kitchen	28	29	30	31	32	33	34
	35	36	37	38	39		
Fun and Games	40	41	42	43	44	45	46
	47	48	49	50	51	52	
Weather Watch	53	54	55	56	57	58	59
	60	61	62	63	64		
Outer Space	65	66	67	68	69	70	71
	72	73	74	75	76	77	
Celebration Times	78	79	80	81	82	83	84
	85	86	87	88	89		
Animals, Animals	90	91	92	93	94	95	96
	97	98	99	100	101	102	
In the Garden	103	104	105	106	107	108	109
	110	111	112	113	114		
The Beautiful Sea	115	116	117	118	119	120	121
	122	123	124	125	126	127	128

Red numbers indicate **Test Your Skills pages.**

©2005 by Evan-Moor Corp. • EMC 4546 • Math

Math • EMC 4546 • ©2005 by Evan-Moor Corp.

Answer Key

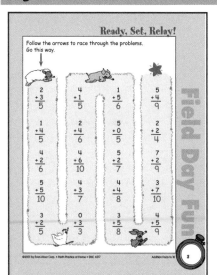

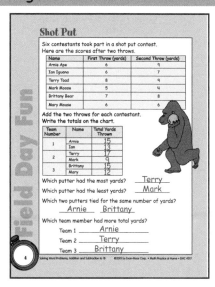

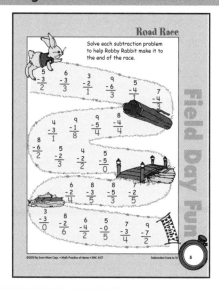

Page 4 — Shot Put

Six contestants took part in a shot put contest. Here are the scores after two throws.

Name	First Throw (yards)	Second Throw (yards)
Arnie Ape	6	9
Ian Iguana	6	7
Terry Toad	8	9
Mark Moose	5	4
Brittany Bear	7	8
Mary Mouse	6	6

Add the two throws for each contestant. Write the totals on the chart.

Team Number	Name	Total Yards Thrown
1	Arnie	15
	Ian	13
2	Terry	17
	Mark	9
3	Brittany	15
	Mary	12

Which putter had the most yards? __Terry__

Which putter had the least yards? __Mark__

Which two putters tied for the same number of yards? __Arnie__ __Brittany__

Which team member had more total yards?

Team 1 __Arnie__

Team 2 __Terry__

Team 3 __Brittany__

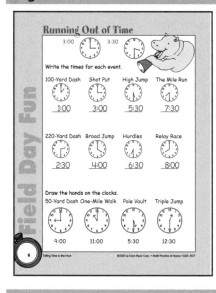

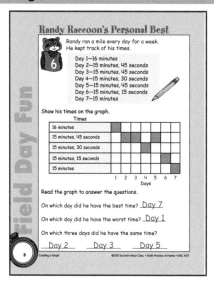

Page 8 — Randy Raccoon's Personal Best

Randy ran a mile every day for a week. He kept track of his times.

Day 1—16 minutes
Day 2—15 minutes, 45 seconds
Day 3—15 minutes, 45 seconds
Day 4—15 minutes, 30 seconds
Day 5—15 minutes, 45 seconds
Day 6—15 minutes, 15 seconds
Day 7—15 minutes

Read the graph to answer the questions.

On which day did he have the best time? __Day 7__

On which day did he have the worst time? __Day 1__

On which three days did he have the same time?

__Day 2__ __Day 3__ __Day 5__

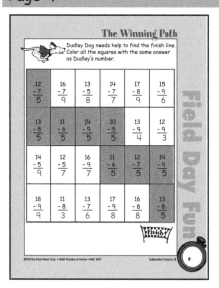

Page 10 — All the Way to the End

Fill in the missing numbers to run the race.

Start

40	69	97	111	357
41	70	98	112	358
42	71	99	113	359
43	72	100	114	360
44	73	101	115	361
45	74	102	116	362
46	75	103	117	363
47	76	104	118	364
48	77	105	119	365
49	78	106	120	366
50	79	107	121	367
51	80	108	122	368
52	81	109	123	369
53	82	110	124	370
54	83	111	125	371

Finish

Page 11 — Ball Toss

Each contestant tossed a ball two times. Write the equation.

$4 + 7 = 11$

$6 + 7 = 13$

$8 + 6 = 14$

$3 + 12 = 15$

$7 + 7 = 14$

$8 + 7 = 15$

©2005 by Evan-Moor Corp. • EMC 4546 • Math

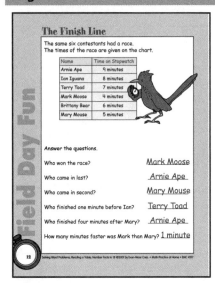

The Finish Line

The same six contestants had a race.
The times of the race are given on the chart.

Name	Time on Stopwatch
Arnie Ape	9 minutes
Ian Iguana	8 minutes
Terry Toad	7 minutes
Mark Moose	4 minutes
Brittany Bear	6 minutes
Mary Mouse	5 minutes

Answer the questions.

Who won the race? **Mark Moose**

Who came in last? **Arnie Ape**

Who came in second? **Mary Mouse**

Who finished one minute before Ian? **Terry Toad**

Who finished four minutes after Mary? **Arnie Ape**

How many minutes faster was Mark than Mary? **1 minute**

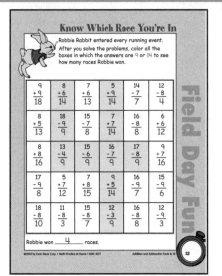

Know Which Race You're In

Robbie Rabbit entered every running event. After you solve the problems, color all the boxes in which the answers are 9 or 14 to see how many races Robbie won.

9 +9 = 18	8 +6 = 14	7 +6 = 13	5 +9 = 14	14 −7 = 7	12 −8 = 4
8 +5 = 13	18 −9 = 9	15 −7 = 8	7 +7 = 14	16 −8 = 8	6 +6 = 12
8 +8 = 16	13 −4 = 9	15 −6 = 9	16 −7 = 9	17 −8 = 9	9 +7 = 16
17 −9 = 8	5 +7 = 12	7 +8 = 15	9 +5 = 14	16 −9 = 7	15 −9 = 6
18 −8 = 10	11 −8 = 3	15 −8 = 7	12 −3 = 9	16 −8 = 8	12 −9 = 3

Robbie won **4** races.

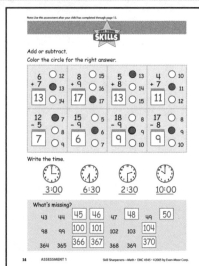

Note: Use this assessment after your child has completed through page 13.

SKILLS

Add or subtract.
Color the circle for the right answer.

6 +7 = 13	8 +9 = 17	5 +8 = 13	4 +7 = 11
12 −5 = 7	15 −9 = 6	18 −9 = 9	17 −8 = 9

Write the time.

3:00   **6:30**   **2:30**   **10:00**

What's missing?

43	44	45	46	47	48	49	50
98	99	100	101	102	103	104	
364	365	366	367	368	369	370	

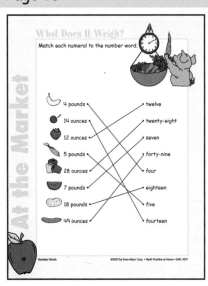

What's in the Shopping Cart?

When you add three or more numbers, it's easier to add pairs of numbers first.

Add.

Answers: 11, 16, 12, 19, 16, 15, 13, 12, 14

Enough Money?

Example: Jan is going to the store. She has 15¢. She wants to buy two pieces of candy. The candy costs 7¢ each. Does she have enough money?
yes Show why. 7 + 7 = 14; 14 is less than 15

Ryan has 18¢. He wants to buy three cookies. Each cookie costs 6¢. Does he have enough money?
Yes Show why. 6 + 6 + 6 = 18

Crystal has 14¢. She wants to buy 4 gumballs. Each gumball costs 4¢. Does she have enough money?
No Show why. 4 + 4 + 4 + 4 = 16

Chris wants to buy 2 packs of baseball cards. Each pack costs 10¢. He only has 18¢. How much more money does he need?
2¢ Show why. 10 + 10 = 20   20 − 18 = 2

John wants to buy 4 jawbreakers. He has 10¢. Each jawbreaker costs 3¢. How much more money does he need?
2¢ Show why. 3 + 3 + 3 + 3 = 12   12 − 10 = 2

Jill wants to buy 5 suckers. Each sucker costs 5¢. She has a quarter. Does she have enough money?
Yes Show why. 5 + 5 + 5 + 5 = 25

How Many Groceries?

Here's another way to solve column addition problems—Look for the two numbers that add up to 10.
Add.

Answers: 16, 16, 16, 16, 15, 12, 17, 12, 16, 20, 18, 18

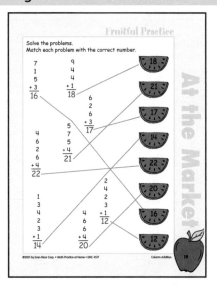

What Does It Weigh?

Match each numeral to the number word.

4 pounds — twelve
14 ounces — twenty-eight
12 ounces — seven
5 pounds — forty-nine
28 ounces — four
7 pounds — eighteen
18 pounds — five
49 ounces — fourteen

Fruitful Practice

Solve the problems.
Match each problem with the correct number.

| 7 1 5 +3 = 16 | 9 4 +1 = 18 |

(watermelon answers: 18, 21, 17, 14, 22, 20, 16, 12)

Money Counts

How much money is in each set of coins?

= 50 ¢
= 50 ¢
= 20 ¢
= 75 ¢
= 55 ¢

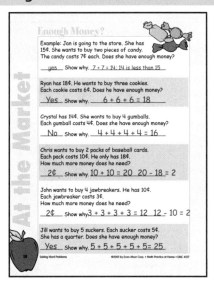

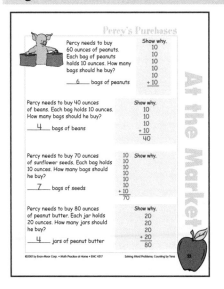

Page 21 — Percy's Purchases

Percy needs to buy 60 ounces of peanuts. Each bag of peanuts holds 10 ounces. How many bags should he buy?
6 bags of peanuts
Show why. 10 + 10 + 10 + 10 + 10 + 10 = 60

Percy needs to buy 40 ounces of beans. Each bag holds 10 ounces. How many bags should he buy?
4 bags of beans
Show why. 10 + 10 + 10 + 10 = 40

Percy needs to buy 70 ounces of sunflower seeds. Each bag holds 10 ounces. How many bags should he buy?
7 bags of seeds
Show why. 10 + 10 + 10 + 10 + 10 + 10 + 10 = 70

Percy needs to buy 80 ounces of peanut butter. Each jar holds 20 ounces. How many jars should he buy?
4 jars of peanut butter
Show why. 20 + 20 + 20 + 20 = 80

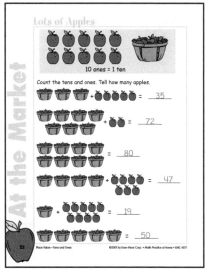

Page 22 — Lots of Apples

10 ones = 1 ten

Count the tens and ones. Tell how many apples.
= **35**
= **72**
= **80**
= **47**
= **19**
= **50**

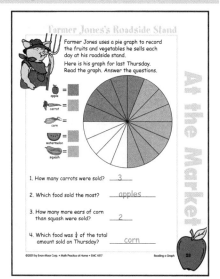

Page 23 — Farmer Jones's Roadside Stand

Farmer Jones uses a pie graph to record the fruits and vegetables he sells each day at his roadside stand.

Here is his graph for last Thursday. Read the graph. Answer the questions.

apple, carrot, corn, watermelon, squash

1. How many carrots were sold? **3**
2. Which food sold the most? **apples**
3. How many more ears of corn than squash were sold? **2**
4. Which food was ¼ of the total amount sold on Thursday? **corn**

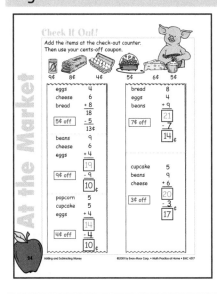

Page 24 — Check It Out!

Add the items at the check-out counter. Then use your cents-off coupon.

eggs 4
cheese 9
bread + 8
18
5¢ off − 5
13¢

beans 9
cheese 6
eggs + 4
19
9¢ off − 9
10¢

popcorn 5
cupcake 5
eggs + 4
14
4¢ off − 4
10

bread 8
eggs 4
beans + 9
21
7¢ off − 7
14

cupcake 5
beans 9
cheese + 6
20
3¢ off − 3
17

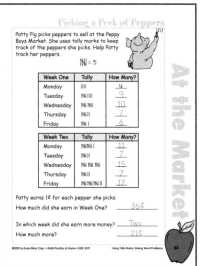

Page 25 — Picking a Peck of Peppers

Patty Pig picks peppers to sell at the Peppy Boys Market. She uses tally marks to keep track of the peppers she picks. Help Patty track her peppers.

||||| = 5

Week One	Tally	How Many?
Monday	||||	4
Tuesday	||||| ||||	9
Wednesday	||||| |||||	10
Thursday	||||| ||	7
Friday	|||||		6

Week Two	Tally	How Many?
Monday	||||| |||||		11
Tuesday	||||| ||	7
Wednesday	||||| ||||| |||||	15
Thursday	||||| ||	7
Friday	||||| ||||| ||||| ||	17

Patty earns 1¢ for each pepper she picks.
How much did she earn in Week One? **36¢**
In which week did she earn more money? **Two**
How much more? **21¢**

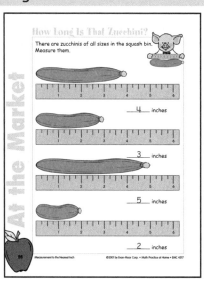

Page 26 — How Long Is That Zucchini?

There are zucchinis of all sizes in the squash bin. Measure them.

4 inches
3 inches
5 inches
2 inches

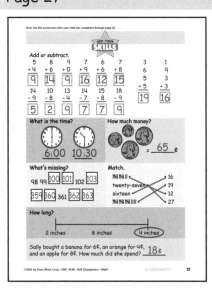

Page 27 — Test Your Skills

Note: Use this assessment after your child has completed through page 26.

Add or subtract.
5 + 4 = **9**
8 + 6 = **14**
9 + 0 = **9**
7 + 9 = **16**
8 + 4 = **12**
7 + 8 = **15**
3 + 6 = **9**
1 + 8 = **9**

14 − 9 = **5**
10 − 8 = **2**
13 − 4 = **9**
14 − 7 = **7**
15 − 8 = **7**
18 − 9 = **9**

What is the time? **6:00** **10:30**

How much money? **65**¢

What's missing?
98 99 **100** **101** 102 **103**
359 **360** 361 **362** 363

Match.
||||| ||||| ||| — 16
twenty-seven
sixteen
||||| ||||| ||||| — 27
— 19
— 12

How long? 2 inches   8 inches   **4 inches**

Sally bought a banana for 6¢, an orange for 4¢, and an apple for 8¢. How much did she spend? **18¢**

Page 28 — What's Cooking?

When you add 2-digit numbers, be sure to add the ones column first.

Find all the answers that have 9 in the ones place. Write the letters of those problems in order on the blank lines. Then you will know what's cooking!

a 21 + 5 = 26
j 11 + 7 = 18
m 23 + 12 = 35
d 33 + 45 = 78
s 35 + 14 = 49
r 21 + 26 = 47
g 30 + 8 = 38

h 52 + 14 = 66
t 16 + 23 = 39
b 63 + 15 = 78
v 55 + 12 = 67
l 32 + 26 = 58
c 91 + 3 = 94
n 44 + 44 = 88

u 62 + 24 = 86
p 77 + 21 = 98
y 63 + 33 = 96
f 80 + 11 = 91
e 21 + 48 = 69
i 15 + 11 = 26
o 74 + 23 = 97

k 34 + 32 = 66
w 22 + 37 = 59
x 64 + 20 = 84
q 24 + 71 = 95
z 42 + 35 = 77

S t e w

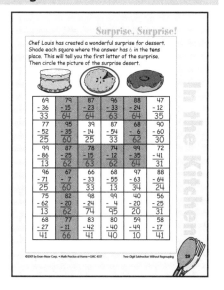

Page 29 — Surprise, Surprise!

Chef Louis has created a wonderful surprise for dessert. Shade each square where the answer has 6 in the tens place. This will tell you the first letter of the surprise. Then circle the picture of the surprise dessert.

69 − 36 = 33
79 − 15 = 64
87 − 23 = 64
96 − 33 = 63
88 − 24 = 64
47 − 12 = 35

77 − 52 = 25
95 − 35 = 60
39 − 14 = 25
87 − 54 = 33
68 − 6 = 62
90 − 60 = 30

99 − 86 = 13
87 − 25 = 62
78 − 15 = 63
74 − 12 = 62
99 − 35 = 64
72 − 41 = 31

96 − 71 = 25
67 − 7 = 60
66 − 33 = 33
68 − 55 = 13
97 − 63 = 34
88 − 64 = 24

75 − 62 = 13
82 − 20 = 62
98 − 24 = 74
99 − 4 = 95
40 − 20 = 20
56 − 25 = 31

68 − 27 = 41
77 − 11 = 66
83 − 42 = 41
80 − 40 = 40
59 − 49 = 10
58 − 17 = 41

Page 30

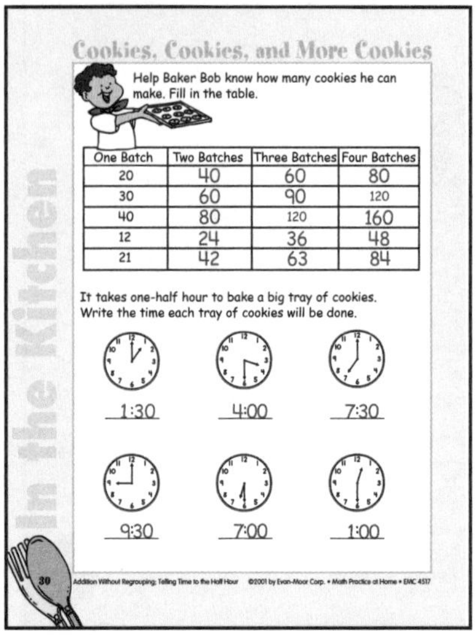

Cookies, Cookies, and More Cookies

Help Baker Bob know how many cookies he can make. Fill in the table.

One Batch	Two Batches	Three Batches	Four Batches
20	40	60	80
30	60	90	120
40	80	120	160
12	24	36	48
21	42	63	84

It takes one-half hour to bake a big tray of cookies. Write the time each tray of cookies will be done.

1:30 4:00 7:30

9:30 7:00 1:00

30 Addition Without Regrouping; Telling Time to the Half Hour ©2001 by Evan-Moor Corp. • Math Practice at Home • EMC 4517

In the Kitchen

Page 31

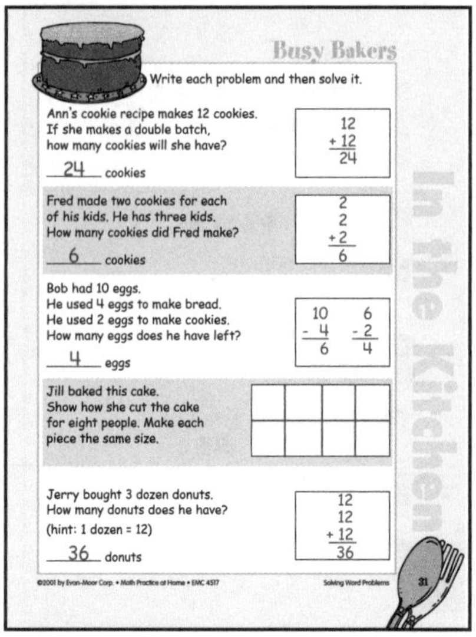

Busy Bakers

Write each problem and then solve it.

Ann's cookie recipe makes 12 cookies. If she makes a double batch, how many cookies will she have?

24 cookies

$12 + 12 = 24$

Fred made two cookies for each of his kids. He has three kids. How many cookies did Fred make?

6 cookies

$2 + 2 + 2 = 6$

Bob had 10 eggs. He used 4 eggs to make bread. He used 2 eggs to make cookies. How many eggs does he have left?

4 eggs

$10 - 4 = 6$ $6 - 2 = 4$

Jill baked this cake. Show how she cut the cake for eight people. Make each piece the same size.

Jerry bought 3 dozen donuts. How many donuts does he have? (hint: 1 dozen = 12)

36 donuts

$12 + 12 + 12 = 36$

©2001 by Evan-Moor Corp. • Math Practice at Home • EMC 4517 Solving Word Problems 31

In the Kitchen

Page 32

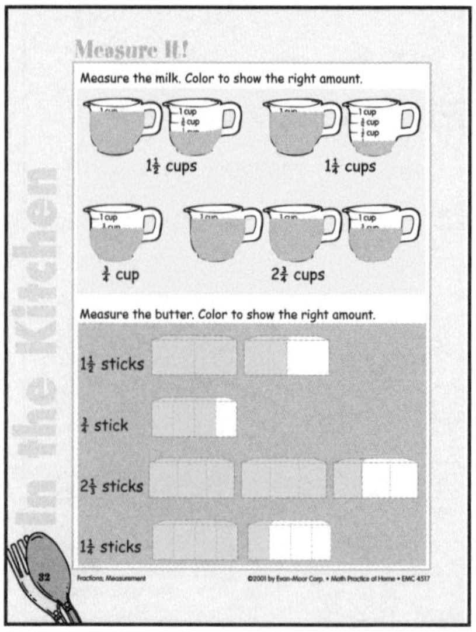

Measure It!

Measure the milk. Color to show the right amount.

$1\frac{1}{2}$ cups $1\frac{1}{4}$ cups

$\frac{3}{4}$ cup $2\frac{3}{4}$ cups

Measure the butter. Color to show the right amount.

$1\frac{1}{2}$ sticks

$\frac{3}{4}$ stick

$2\frac{1}{4}$ sticks

$1\frac{1}{4}$ sticks

32 Fractions; Measurement ©2001 by Evan-Moor Corp. • Math Practice at Home • EMC 4517

In the Kitchen

Page 33

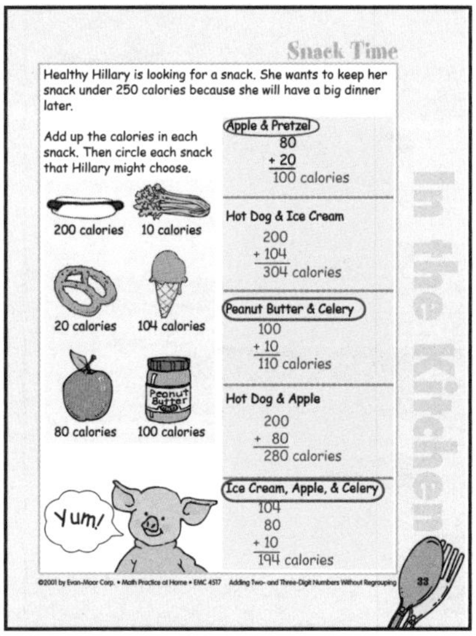

Snack Time

Healthy Hillary is looking for a snack. She wants to keep her snack under 250 calories because she will have a big dinner later.

Add up the calories in each snack. Then circle each snack that Hillary might choose.

200 calories 10 calories

20 calories 104 calories

80 calories 100 calories

Yum!

(Apple & Pretzel) $80 + 20 = 100$ calories

Hot Dog & Ice Cream $200 + 104 = 304$ calories

(Peanut Butter & Celery) $100 + 10 = 110$ calories

Hot Dog & Apple $200 + 80 = 280$ calories

(Ice Cream, Apple, & Celery) $104 + 80 + 10 = 194$ calories

©2001 by Evan-Moor Corp. • Math Practice at Home • EMC 4517 Adding Two- and Three-Digit Numbers Without Regrouping 33

In the Kitchen

Page 34

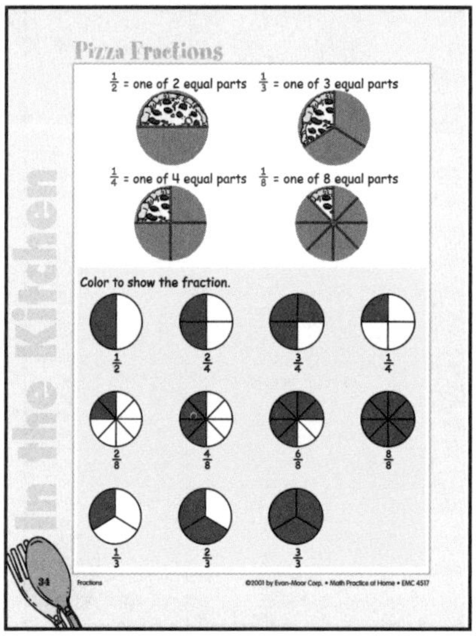

Pizza Fractions

$\frac{1}{2}$ = one of 2 equal parts $\frac{1}{3}$ = one of 3 equal parts

$\frac{1}{4}$ = one of 4 equal parts $\frac{1}{8}$ = one of 8 equal parts

Color to show the fraction.

$\frac{1}{2}$ $\frac{2}{4}$ $\frac{3}{4}$ $\frac{1}{4}$

$\frac{2}{8}$ $\frac{4}{8}$ $\frac{6}{8}$ $\frac{8}{8}$

$\frac{1}{3}$ $\frac{2}{3}$ $\frac{3}{3}$

34 Fractions ©2001 by Evan-Moor Corp. • Math Practice at Home • EMC 4517

In the Kitchen

Page 35

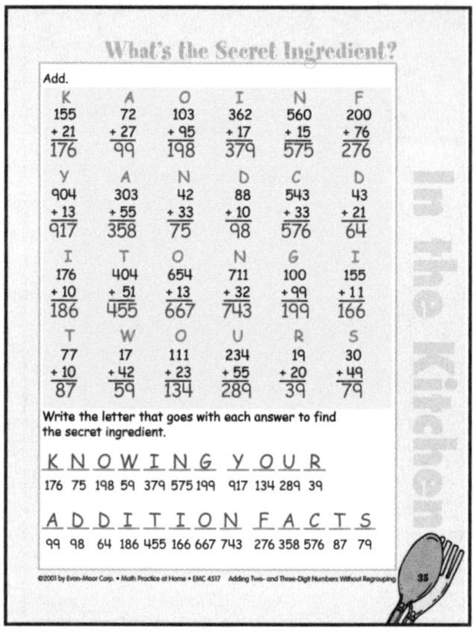

What's the Secret Ingredient?

Add.

K	A	O	I	N	F
155 + 21 = 176	72 + 27 = 99	103 + 95 = 198	362 + 17 = 379	560 + 15 = 575	200 + 76 = 276

Y	A	N	D	C	D
904 + 13 = 917	303 + 55 = 358	42 + 33 = 75	88 + 10 = 98	543 + 33 = 576	43 + 21 = 64

I	T	O	N	G	I
176 + 10 = 186	404 + 51 = 455	654 + 13 = 667	711 + 32 = 743	100 + 99 = 199	155 + 11 = 166

T	W	O	U	R	S
77 + 10 = 87	17 + 42 = 59	111 + 23 = 134	234 + 55 = 289	19 + 20 = 39	30 + 49 = 79

Write the letter that goes with each answer to find the secret ingredient.

K N O W I N G Y O U R

176 75 198 59 379 575 199 917 134 289 39

A D D I T I O N F A C T S

99 98 64 186 455 166 667 743 276 358 576 87 79

©2001 by Evan-Moor Corp. • Math Practice at Home • EMC 4517 Adding Two- and Three-Digit Numbers Without Regrouping 35

In the Kitchen

Page 36

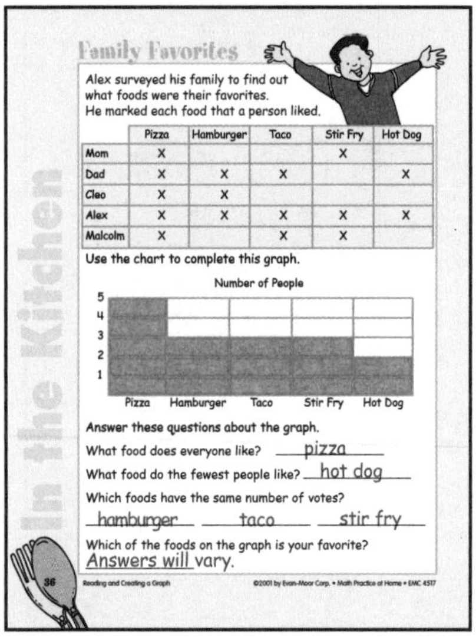

Family Favorites

Alex surveyed his family to find out what foods were their favorites. He marked each food that a person liked.

	Pizza	Hamburger	Taco	Stir Fry	Hot Dog
Mom	X			X	
Dad	X	X	X		X
Cleo	X	X			
Alex	X	X	X	X	X
Malcolm	X		X	X	

Use the chart to complete this graph.

Number of People

Pizza Hamburger Taco Stir Fry Hot Dog

Answer these questions about the graph.

What food does everyone like? pizza

What food do the fewest people like? hot dog

Which foods have the same number of votes?

hamburger taco stir fry

Which of the foods on the graph is your favorite?

Answers will vary.

36 Reading and Creating a Graph ©2001 by Evan-Moor Corp. • Math Practice at Home • EMC 4517

In the Kitchen

Page 37

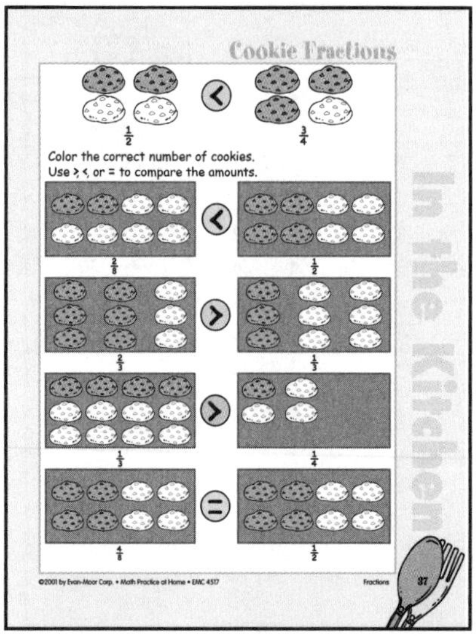

Cookie Fractions

$\frac{1}{2}$ < $\frac{3}{4}$

Color the correct number of cookies. Use >, <, or = to compare the amounts.

$\frac{1}{8}$ < $\frac{1}{2}$

$\frac{2}{3}$ > $\frac{1}{3}$

$\frac{1}{3}$ > $\frac{1}{4}$

$\frac{1}{4}$ = $\frac{1}{2}$

©2001 by Evan-Moor Corp. • Math Practice at Home • EMC 4517 Fractions 37

In the Kitchen

Page 38

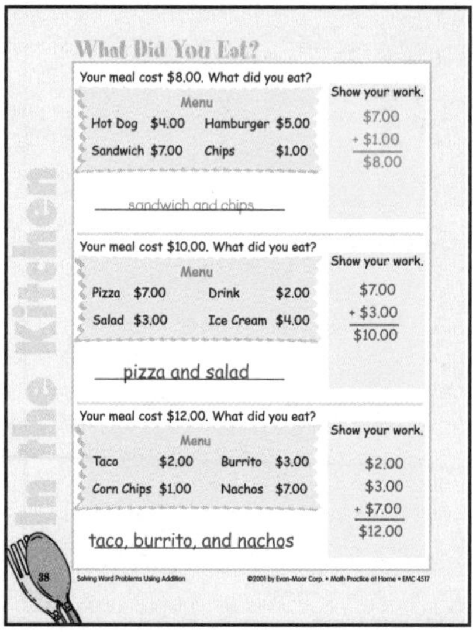

What Did You Eat?

Your meal cost $8.00. What did you eat?

Menu

Hot Dog $4.00 Hamburger $5.00

Sandwich $7.00 Chips $1.00

Show your work. $7.00 + $1.00 = $8.00

sandwich and chips

Your meal cost $10.00. What did you eat?

Menu

Pizza $7.00 Drink $2.00

Salad $3.00 Ice Cream $4.00

Show your work. $7.00 + $3.00 = $10.00

pizza and salad

Your meal cost $12.00. What did you eat?

Menu

Taco $2.00 Burrito $3.00

Corn Chips $1.00 Nachos $7.00

Show your work. $2.00 + $3.00 + $7.00 = $12.00

taco, burrito, and nachos

38 Solving Word Problems Using Addition ©2001 by Evan-Moor Corp. • Math Practice at Home • EMC 4517

In the Kitchen

Math • EMC 4546 • ©2005 by Evan-Moor Corp.

Page 39

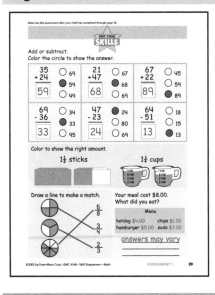

Note: Use this assessment after your child has completed through page 36.

TEST YOUR SKILLS

Add or subtract. Color the circle to show the answer.

35 + 24 = 59 ● 59
21 + 47 = 68 ● 68
67 + 22 = 89 ● 89
69 − 36 = 33 ● 33
47 − 23 = 24 ● 24
64 − 51 = 13 ● 13

Color to show the right amount.

1½ sticks
1½ cups

Draw a line to make a match.

Your meal cost $8.00. What did you eat?

Menu
hotdog $4.00   chips $1.00
hamburger $5.00   soda $2.00

answers may vary

Page 40

Just Ducky!
Why do ducks have big bills?

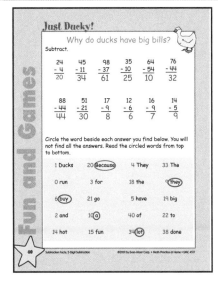

Subtract.

| 24 − 4 = 20 | 45 − 11 = 34 | 98 − 37 = 61 | 35 − 10 = 25 | 64 − 54 = 10 | 76 − 44 = 32 |

| 88 − 44 = 44 | 51 − 21 = 30 | 17 − 9 = 8 | 12 − 6 = 6 | 16 − 9 = 7 | 14 − 5 = 9 |

Circle the word beside each answer you find below. You will not find all the answers. Read the circled words from top to bottom.

1 Ducks	20 Because	4 They	33 The
0 run	3 for	18 the	9 they
6 buy	21 go	5 have	19 big
2 and	10 a	40 of	22 to
14 hot	15 fun	34 lot	38 done

Page 41

Just the Same
If you draw a line through the middle of something and both sides are the same, the object is symmetrical.
Draw to make the pictures symmetrical.

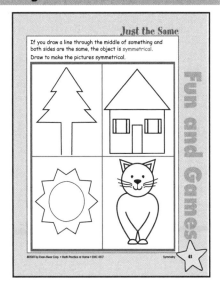

Page 42

Can You Believe Your Eyes?
Color answers that end in:

0 green   2 purple   4 red
1 blue   3 violet   5 orange

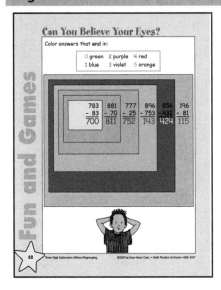

| 783 − 83 = 700 | 881 − 70 = 811 | 777 − 25 = 752 | 896 − 753 = 143 | 856 − 432 = 424 | 196 − 81 = 115 |

Page 43

Which Ride?

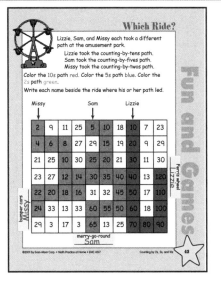

Lizzie, Sam, and Missy each took a different path at the amusement park.
Lizzie took the counting-by-tens path.
Sam took the counting-by-fives path.
Missy took the counting-by-twos path.
Color the 10s path red. Color the 5s path blue. Color the 2s path green.
Write each name beside the ride where his or her path led.

Missy   Sam   Lizzie

2	9	11	25	5	10	18	10	7	23
4	6	8	27	29	15	19	20	9	29
21	25	10	30	25	20	21	30	11	30
23	27	12	14	30	35	40	40	13	120
22	20	18	16	31	32	45	50	17	110
24	33	13	33	60	55	50	60	18	100
29	3	17	3	65	13	25	70	80	90

Ferris wheel Lizzie
bumper cars Missy
merry-go-round Sam

Page 44

Basketball Pointers

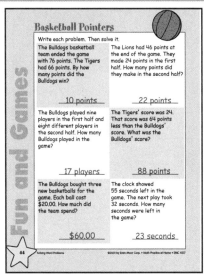

Write each problem. Then solve it.

The Bulldogs basketball team ended the game with 76 points. The Tigers had 66 points. By how many points did the Bulldogs win?

10 points

The Lions had 46 points at the end of the game. They made 24 points in the first half. How many points did they make in the second half?

22 points

The Bulldogs played nine players in the first half and eight different players in the second half. How many Bulldogs played in the game?

17 players

The Tigers' score was 24. That score was 64 points less than the Bulldogs' score. What was the Bulldogs' score?

88 points

The Bulldogs bought three new basketballs for the game. Each ball cost $20.00. How much did the team spend?

$60.00

The clock showed 55 seconds left in the game. The next play took 32 seconds. How many seconds were left in the game?

23 seconds

Page 45

Round Up the Bucks

Cowboy Dan is fixin' to lasso some money to buy some new duds.
Circle the amount of money needed to buy each thing.

$5.55 $1.25
$2.35 $4.75

Page 46

A Goofy Riddle
What can you wear that everyone will like?

| A − 24 | E − 22 | G − 53 | R − 45 |
| B − 35 | I − 12 | N − 16 | T − 17 |

| 87 − 63 = 24 | 68 − 15 = 53 | 89 − 44 = 45 | 59 − 37 = 22 | 78 − 54 = 24 | 78 − 61 = 17 |
| A | G | R | E | A | T |

| 69 − 34 = 35 | 74 − 62 = 12 | 99 − 46 = 53 | 87 − 34 = 53 | 56 − 11 = 45 | 48 − 36 = 12 | 99 − 83 = 16 |
| B | I | G | G | R | I | N |

Draw the answer here.

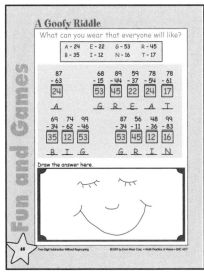

Page 47

Cross the River

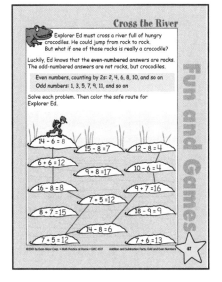

Explorer Ed must cross a river full of hungry crocodiles. He could jump from rock to rock. But what if one of those rocks is really a crocodile?

Luckily, Ed knows that the even-numbered answers are rocks. The odd-numbered answers are not rocks, but crocodiles.

Even numbers, counting by 2s: 2, 4, 6, 8, 10, and so on
Odd numbers: 1, 3, 5, 7, 9, 11, and so on

Solve each problem. Then color the safe route for Explorer Ed.

14 − 6 = 8   15 − 8 = 7   12 − 8 = 4
6 + 6 = 12   10 − 6 = 4
16 − 8 = 8   9 + 8 = 17
9 + 7 = 16
8 + 7 = 15   7 + 5 = 12   18 − 9 = 9
7 + 5 = 12   14 − 8 = 6
7 + 6 = 13

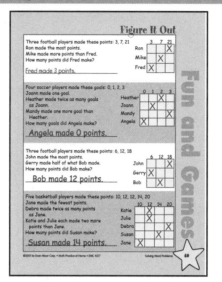

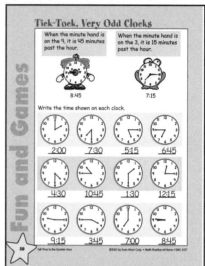

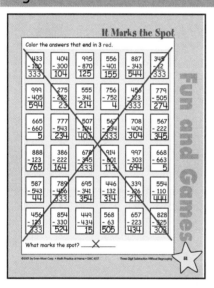

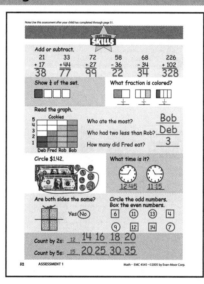

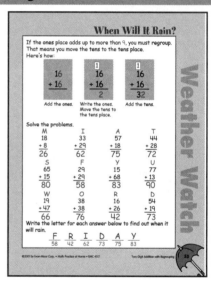

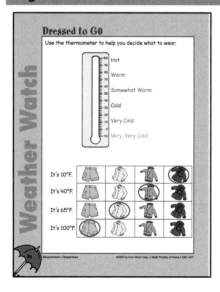

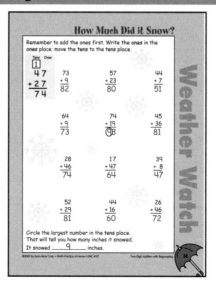

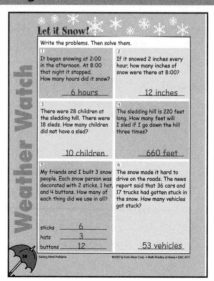

Page 57
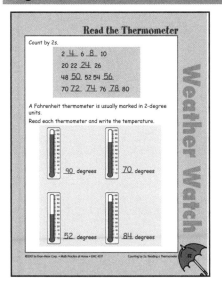

Read the Thermometer

Count by 2s.

2 4 6 8 10
20 22 24 26
48 50 52 54 56
70 72 74 76 78 80

A Fahrenheit thermometer is usually marked in 2-degree units.

Read each thermometer and write the temperature.

90 degrees   70 degrees
52 degrees   84 degrees

Page 58
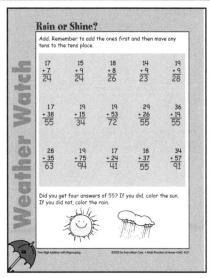

Rain or Shine?

Add. Remember to add the ones first and then move any tens to the tens place.

17 + 7 = 24   15 + 9 = 24   18 + 8 = 26   14 + 9 = 23   19 + 9 = 28

17 + 38 = 55   19 + 15 = 34   19 + 53 = 72   29 + 26 = 55   36 + 19 = 55

28 + 35 = 63   19 + 75 = 94   17 + 24 = 41   18 + 37 = 55   34 + 57 = 91

Did you get four answers of 55? If you did, color the sun. If you did not, color the rain.

Page 59

Foul-Weather Gear

Color to show the fractions.

1/2   1/3   1/4   2/3   4/4

Page 60
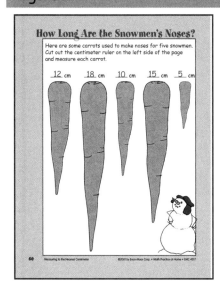

How Long Are the Snowmen's Noses?

Here are some carrots used to make noses for five snowmen. Cut out the centimeter ruler on the left side of the page and measure each carrot.

12 cm   18 cm   10 cm   15 cm   5 cm

Page 61
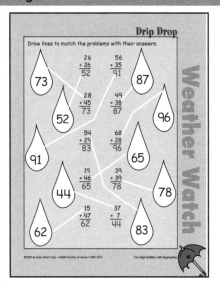

Drip Drop

Draw lines to match the problems with their answers.

73   52   91   44   62
87   96   65   78   83

26 + 26 = 52   56 + 35 = 91
28 + 45 = 73   49 + 38 = 87
54 + 29 = 83   68 + 28 = 96
19 + 46 = 65   39 + 39 = 78
15 + 47 = 62   37 + 7 = 44

Page 62
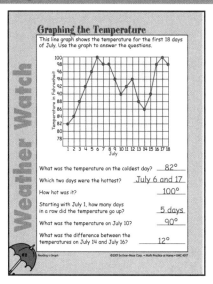

Graphing the Temperature

This line graph shows the temperature for the first 18 days of July. Use the graph to answer the questions.

What was the temperature on the coldest day?   82°
Which two days were the hottest?   July 6 and 17
How hot was it?   100°
Starting with July 1, how many days in a row did the temperature go up?   5 days
What was the temperature on July 10?   90°
What was the difference between the temperatures on July 14 and July 16?   12°

Page 63
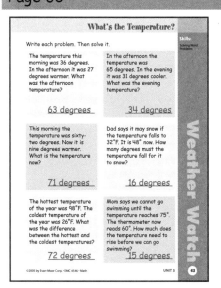

What's the Temperature?

Write each problem. Then solve it.

The temperature this morning was 36 degrees. In the afternoon it was 27 degrees warmer. What was the afternoon temperature?   63 degrees

In the afternoon the temperature was 65 degrees. In the evening it was 31 degrees cooler. What was the evening temperature?   34 degrees

This morning the temperature was sixty-two degrees. Now it is nine degrees warmer. What is the temperature now?   71 degrees

Dad says it may snow if the temperature falls to 32°F. It is 48° now. How many degrees must the temperature fall for it to snow?   16 degrees

The hottest temperature of the year was 98°F. The coldest temperature of the year was 26°F. What was the difference between the hottest and the coldest temperatures?   72 degrees

Mom says we cannot go swimming until the temperature reaches 75°. The thermometer now reads 60°. How much does the temperature need to rise before we can go swimming?   15 degrees

Page 64
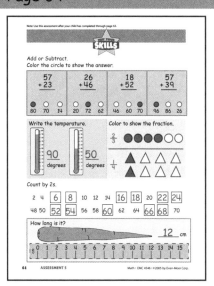

SKILLS

Add or Subtract. Color the circle to show the answer.

57 + 23 = 80   26 + 46 = 72   18 + 52 = 70   57 + 39 = 96

Write the temperature.   90 degrees   50 degrees

Color to show the fraction.   2/5   1/4

Count by 2s.

2 4 6 8 10 12 14 16 18 20 22 24
48 50 52 54 56 58 60 62 64 66 68 70

How long is it?   12 cm

Page 65
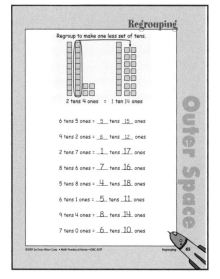

Regrouping

Regroup to make one less set of tens.

2 tens 4 ones = 1 ten 14 ones

6 tens 5 ones = 5 tens 15 ones
9 tens 2 ones = 8 tens 12 ones
2 tens 7 ones = 1 ten 17 ones
8 tens 6 ones = 7 tens 16 ones
5 tens 8 ones = 4 tens 18 ones
6 tens 1 ones = 5 tens 11 ones
9 tens 4 ones = 8 tens 14 ones
7 tens 0 ones = 6 tens 10 ones

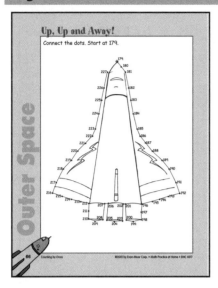

Up, Up and Away!

Connect the dots. Start at 179.

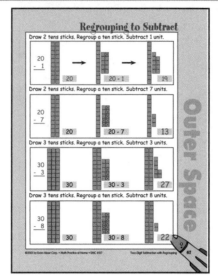

Regrouping to Subtract

Draw 2 tens sticks. Regroup a ten stick. Subtract 1 unit.

20 − 1 → 20 → 20 − 1 → 19

Draw 2 tens sticks. Regroup a ten stick. Subtract 7 units.

20 − 7 → 20 → 20 − 7 → 13

Draw 3 tens sticks. Regroup a ten stick. Subtract 3 units.

30 − 3 → 30 → 30 − 3 → 27

Draw 3 tens sticks. Regroup a ten stick. Subtract 8 units.

30 − 8 → 30 → 30 − 8 → 22

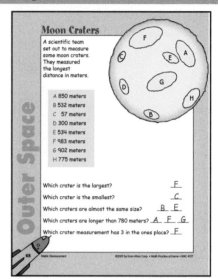

Moon Craters

A scientific team set out to measure some moon craters. They measured the longest distance in meters.

A 850 meters
B 532 meters
C 57 meters
D 300 meters
E 534 meters
F 983 meters
G 902 meters
H 775 meters

Which crater is the largest? F

Which crater is the smallest? C

Which craters are almost the same size? B E

Which craters are longer than 780 meters? A F G

Which crater measurement has 3 in the ones place? F

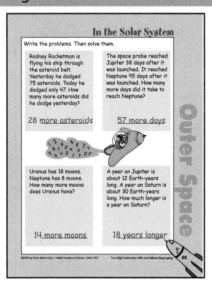

In the Solar System

Write the problems. Then solve them.

Rodney Rocketman is flying his ship through the asteroid belt. Yesterday he dodged 75 asteroids. Today he dodged only 47. How many more asteroids did he dodge yesterday?

28 more asteroids

The space probe reached Jupiter 38 days after it was launched. It reached Neptune 95 days after it was launched. How many more days did it take to reach Neptune?

57 more days

Uranus has 18 moons. Neptune has 8 moons. How many more moons does Uranus have?

14 more moons

A year on Jupiter is about 12 Earth-years long. A year on Saturn is about 30 Earth-years long. How much longer is a year on Saturn?

18 years longer

Subtraction with Regrouping

This is what I think when I need to regroup to subtract:
I can't take 6 away from 4, so I must regroup the tens.
Now I have 2 tens and 14 ones.
14 − 6 = 8
2 tens − 0 tens = 2 tens

34 − 6 = 28

30 − 3 = 27   51 − 8 = 43   43 − 5 = 38   50 − 7 = 43   28 − 9 = 19

74 − 5 = 69   30 − 1 = 29   34 − 9 = 25   42 − 3 = 39   23 − 6 = 17

21 − 5 = 16   64 − 9 = 55   55 − 8 = 47   31 − 5 = 26   77 − 9 = 68

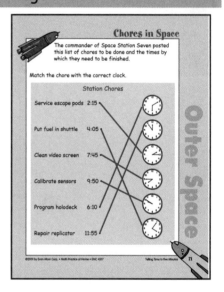

Chores in Space

The commander of Space Station Seven posted this list of chores to be done and the times by which they need to be finished.

Match the chore with the correct clock.

Station Chores

Service escape pods 2:15
Put fuel in shuttle 4:05
Clean video screen 7:45
Calibrate sensors 9:50
Program holodeck 6:10
Repair replicator 11:55

Riddle Time

If athletes get athlete's foot, what do astronauts get?

e - 39   l - 62   t - 47
g - 78   m - 36   y - 24
h - 56   o - 89
i - 17   s - 29

91 − 44 = 47   82 − 26 = 56   77 − 38 = 39   63 − 39 = 24
T   H   E   Y

96 − 18 = 78   96 − 57 = 39   93 − 46 = 47
G   E   T

95 − 59 = 36   75 − 58 = 17   50 − 25 = 25   80 − 55 = 25   80 − 18 = 62   64 − 25 = 39
M   I   S   S   L   E

84 − 37 = 47   98 − 9 = 89   52 − 13 = 39
T   O   E

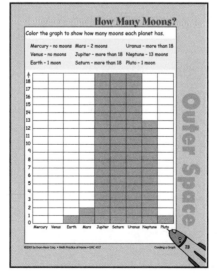

How Many Moons?

Color the graph to show how many moons each planet has.

Mercury - no moons   Mars - 2 moons   Uranus - more than 18
Venus - no moons   Jupiter - more than 18   Neptune - 13 moons
Earth - 1 moon   Saturn - more than 18   Pluto - 1 moon

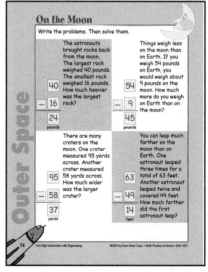

On the Moon

Write the problems. Then solve them.

The astronauts brought rocks back from the moon. The largest rock weighed 40 pounds. The smallest rock weighed 16 pounds. How much heavier was the largest rock?

40 − 16 = 24 pounds

Things weigh less on the moon than on Earth. If you weigh 54 pounds on Earth, you would weigh about 9 pounds on the moon. How much more do you weigh on Earth than on the moon?

54 − 9 = 45 pounds

There are many craters on the moon. One crater measured 95 yards across. Another crater measured 58 yards across. How much wider was the larger crater?

95 − 58 = 37 yards

You can leap much farther on the moon than on Earth. One astronaut leaped three times for a total of 63 feet. Another astronaut leaped twice and covered 49 feet. How much farther did the first astronaut leap?

63 − 49 = 14 feet

138

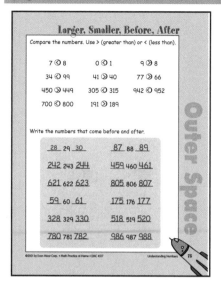

Larger, Smaller, Before, After

Compare the numbers. Use > (greater than) or < (less than).

7 < 8   0 < 1   9 > 8

34 < 99   41 > 40   77 > 66

450 > 449   305 < 315   942 < 952

700 < 800   191 > 189

Write the numbers that come before and after.

_28_ 29 _30_   _87_ 88 _89_

_242_ 243 _244_   _459_ 460 _461_

_621_ 622 _623_   _805_ 806 _807_

_59_ 60 _61_   _175_ 176 _177_

_328_ 329 _330_   _518_ 519 _520_

_780_ 781 _782_   _986_ 987 _988_

Space Tie-Tac-Toe

Mark an X on problems where you had to regroup.
Mark an O on problems with no regrouping.

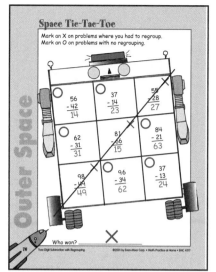

56 − 42 = 14	37 − 14 = 23	55 − 28 = 27
62 − 31 = 31	81 − 66 = 15	84 − 21 = 63
98 − 49 = 49	96 − 34 = 62	37 − 13 = 24

Who won? __X__

SKILLS

Add or subtract. You may or may not need to regroup.

15 + 15 = 30   12 + 29 = 41   34 − 16 = 18   86 − 16 = 70   42 + 17 = 59   41 − 39 = 2

Read the thermometer.

Is it hot? ○ Yes ● No

What is the temperature?
__50__ degrees Fahrenheit

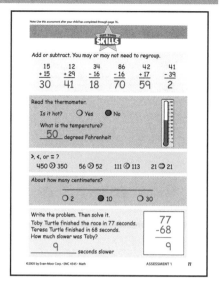

>, <, or = ?

450 > 350   56 > 52   111 < 113   21 = 21

About how many centimeters?

○ 2   ● 10   ○ 30

Write the problem. Then solve it.
Toby Turtle finished the race in 77 seconds.
Teresa Turtle finished in 68 seconds.
How much slower was Toby?

__9__ seconds slower

77 − 68 = 9

Celebration Times

Add. Remember—if the ones are greater than 9, you must regroup and move the tens to the tens place.

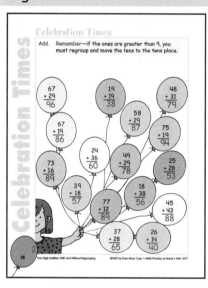

67 + 29 = 96   19 + 19 = 38   48 + 31 = 79

67 + 19 = 86   58 + 29 = 87   75 + 19 = 94

24 + 36 = 60   49 + 29 = 78   25 + 28 = 53

73 + 16 = 89   39 + 18 = 57   18 + 38 = 56

77 + 12 = 89   45 + 43 = 88

37 + 28 = 65   26 + 14 = 40

Pretty Presents

The distance around something is called the perimeter.
How far is it around each shape?

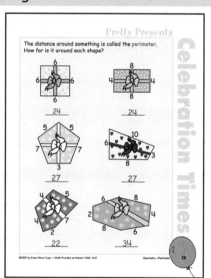

6, 6, 6, 6 → 24

8, 4, 8, 4 → 24

7, 6, 7, 7 → 27

10, 6, 8, 3 → 27

4, 5, 4, 5, 4 → 22

5, 8, 8, 2, 4, 7 → 34

Ring in the New!

Subtract. Remember, if there are not enough ones to subtract, regroup the tens to make more ones.

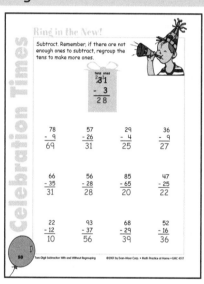

3 ̶4 ̶1 − 3 = 28

78 − 9 = 69   57 − 26 = 31   29 − 4 = 25   36 − 9 = 27

66 − 35 = 31   56 − 28 = 28   85 − 65 = 20   47 − 25 = 22

22 − 12 = 10   93 − 37 = 56   68 − 29 = 39   52 − 16 = 36

You're Having a Party!

Here are the prices of some items you might want to have at your party. Use the information to help you write and solve each problem.

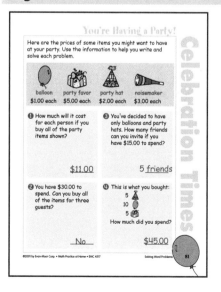

balloon $1.00 each   party favor $5.00 each   party hat $2.00 each   noisemaker $3.00 each

❶ How much will it cost for each person if you buy all of the party items shown? __$11.00__

❷ You have $30.00 to spend. Can you buy all of the items for three guests? __No__

❸ You've decided to have only balloons and party hats. How many friends can you invite if you have $15.00 to spend? __5__ friends

❹ This is what you bought:
5 🎉
10 🎈
5 🎩
How much did you spend? __$45.00__

Here Comes the Parade

We saw these things in the parade:

7 bands   12 clowns
4 dogs   10 floats
11 funny cars   9 bicycles
5 balloons   8 horses
3 fire trucks

Label the graph and color in the sections to show the information above.

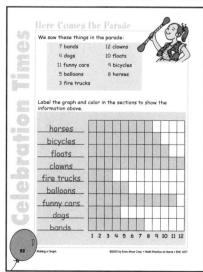

horses
bicycles
floats
clowns
fire trucks
balloons
funny cars
dogs
bands

1 2 3 4 5 6 7 8 9 10 11 12

Who Am I?

I may promise you a treasure, but watch out! I'm tricky.

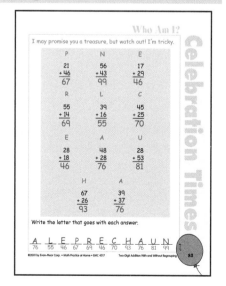

P: 21 + 46 = 67
N: 56 + 43 = 99
E: 17 + 29 = 46

R: 55 + 14 = 69
L: 39 + 16 = 55
C: 45 + 25 = 70

E: 28 + 18 = 46
A: 48 + 28 = 76
U: 28 + 53 = 81

H: 67 + 26 = 93
A: 39 + 37 = 76

Write the letter that goes with each answer.

A L E P R E C H A U N
76 55 46 67 69 46 70 93 76 81 99

Page 84

Page 85

Page 86

Page 87

Page 88

Page 89

Page 90

Page 91

Page 92

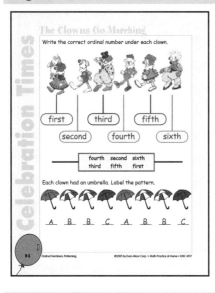

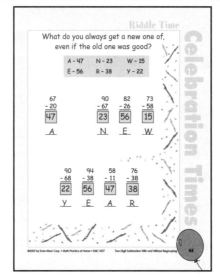

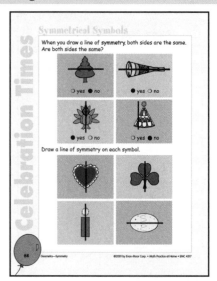

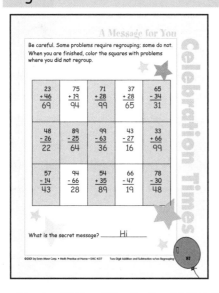

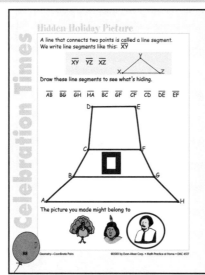

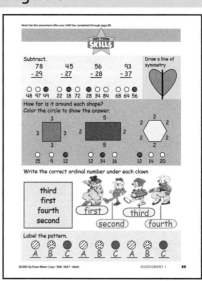

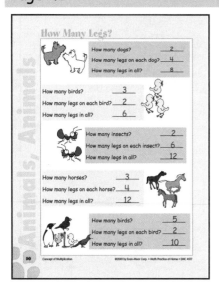

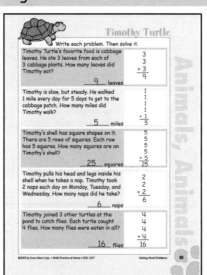

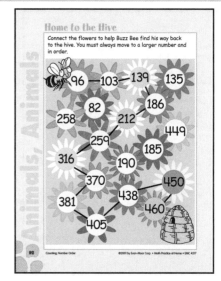

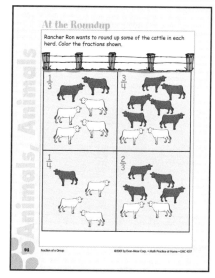

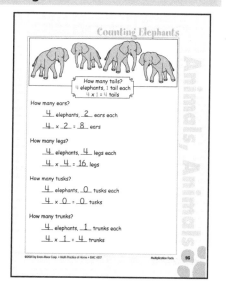

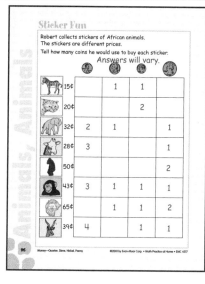

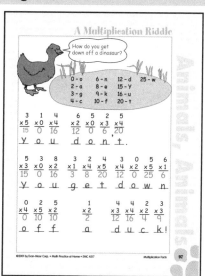

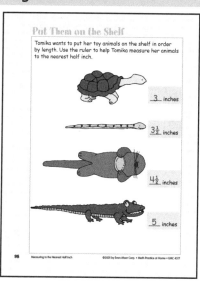

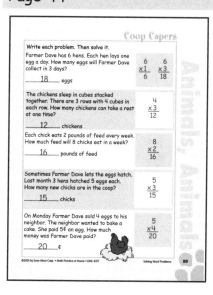

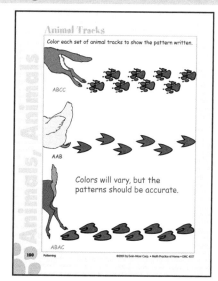

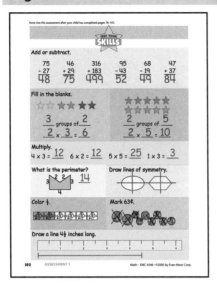

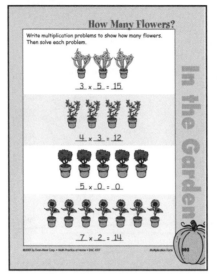

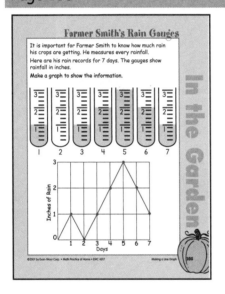

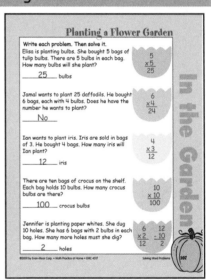

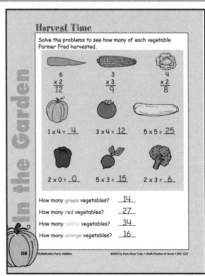

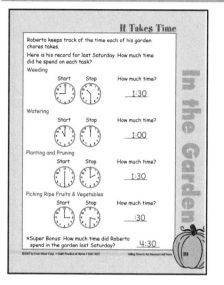

It Takes Time

Roberto keeps track of the time each of his garden chores takes.

Here is his record for last Saturday. How much time did he spend on each task?

Weeding
Start / Stop / How much time? — 1:30

Watering
Start / Stop / How much time? — 1:00

Planting and Pruning
Start / Stop / How much time? — 1:30

Picking Ripe Fruits & Vegetables
Start / Stop / How much time? — :30

★Super Bonus: How much time did Roberto spend in the garden last Saturday? 4:30

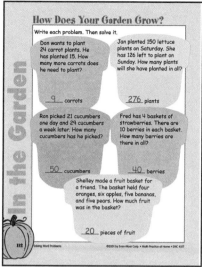

How Does Your Garden Grow?

Write each problem. Then solve it.

Don wants to plant 24 carrot plants. He has planted 15. How many more carrots does he need to plant? — 9 carrots

Jan planted 150 lettuce plants on Saturday. She has 126 left to plant on Sunday. How many plants will she have planted in all? — 276 plants

Ron picked 21 cucumbers one day and 29 cucumbers a week later. How many cucumbers has he picked? — 50 cucumbers

Fred has 4 baskets of strawberries. There are 10 berries in each basket. How many berries are there in all? — 40 berries

Shelley made a fruit basket for a friend. The basket held four oranges, six apples, five bananas, and five pears. How much fruit was in the basket? — 20 pieces of fruit

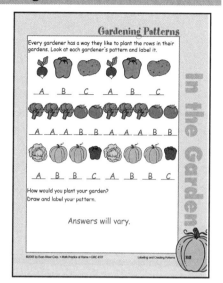

Gardening Patterns

Every gardener has a way they like to plant the rows in their gardens. Look at each gardener's pattern and label it.

A B C A B C

A A A B B B A A A B B

A B B C A B B C

How would you plant your garden? Draw and label your pattern.

Answers will vary.

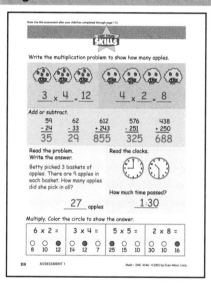

SKILLS

Write the multiplication problem to show how many apples.

3 x 4 = 12   4 x 2 = 8

Add or subtract.

59 − 24 = 35   62 − 33 = 29   612 + 243 = 855   576 − 251 = 325   438 + 250 = 688

Read the problem. Write the answer.
Betty picked 3 baskets of apples. There are 9 apples in each basket. How many apples did she pick in all? — 27 apples

Read the clocks. How much time passed? — 1:30

Multiply. Color the circle to show the answer.
6 x 2 = 12   3 x 4 = 12   5 x 5 = 25   2 x 8 = 16

ASSESSMENT 1

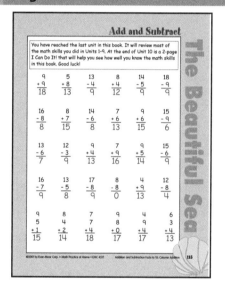

Add and Subtract

You have reached the last unit in this book. It will review most of the math skills you did in Units 1–9. At the end of Unit 10 is a 2-page I Can Do It! that will help you see how well you know the math skills in this book. Good luck!

9 + 9 = 18   5 + 8 = 13   13 − 4 = 9   8 + 4 = 12   14 − 5 = 9   18 − 9 = 9

16 − 8 = 8   8 + 7 = 15   14 − 6 = 8   7 + 6 = 13   9 + 6 = 15   15 − 9 = 6

13 − 6 = 7   12 − 3 = 9   9 + 4 = 13   7 + 9 = 16   9 + 5 = 14   15 − 6 = 9

16 − 7 = 9   13 − 5 = 8   17 − 8 = 9   8 − 8 = 0   4 + 9 = 13   12 − 8 = 4

9 + 5 + 1 = 15   8 + 4 + 2 = 14   7 + 7 + 4 = 18   9 + 8 + 0 = 17   9 + 4 + 4 = 17   6 + 3 + 4 = 13

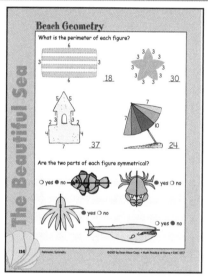

Beach Geometry

What is the perimeter of each figure? — 18, 30, 37, 24

Are the two parts of each figure symmetrical?
● yes ○ no
○ yes ● no
● yes ○ no
○ yes ● no

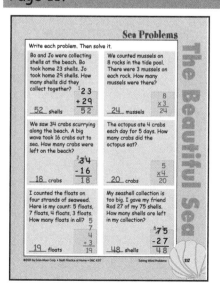

Sea Problems

Write each problem. Then solve it.

Bo and Jo were collecting shells at the beach. Bo took home 23 shells. Jo took home 29 shells. How many shells did they collect together? 23 + 29 = 52 shells

We counted mussels on 8 rocks in the tide pool. There were 3 mussels on each rock. How many mussels were there? 8 x 3 = 24 mussels

We saw 34 crabs scurrying along the beach. A big wave took 16 crabs out to sea. How many crabs were left on the beach? 34 − 16 = 18 crabs

The octopus ate 4 crabs each day for 5 days. How many crabs did the octopus eat? 5 x 4 = 20 crabs

I counted the floats on four strands of seaweed. Here is my count: 5 floats, 7 floats, 4 floats, 3 floats. How many floats in all? 5 + 7 + 4 + 3 = 19 floats

My seashell collection is too big. I gave my friend Rod 27 of my 75 shells. How many shells are left in my collection? 75 − 27 = 48 shells

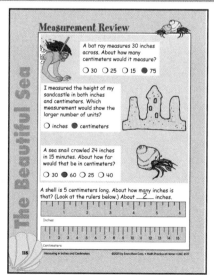

Measurement Review

A bat ray measures 30 inches across. About how many centimeters would it measure? ○ 30 ○ 25 ○ 15 ● 75

I measured the height of my sandcastle in both inches and centimeters. Which measurement would show the larger number of units? ○ inches ● centimeters

A sea snail crawled 24 inches in 15 minutes. About how far would that be in centimeters? ○ 30 ● 60 ○ 25 ○ 10

A shell is 5 centimeters long. About how many inches is that? (Look at the rulers below.) About 2 inches.

Two-Digit Addition and Subtraction

20 + 60 = 80   19 + 22 = 41   55 + 35 = 90   10 + 81 = 91   29 + 39 = 68

38 − 21 = 17   44 − 32 = 12   32 − 13 = 19   43 − 27 = 16   97 − 19 = 78   45 − 26 = 19

72 − 27 = 45   66 + 26 = 92   52 + 47 = 99   66 − 22 = 44   43 − 29 = 14   55 − 49 = 6

77 − 27 = 50   76 + 18 = 94   38 + 27 = 65   30 − 11 = 19   33 − 25 = 8   80 − 11 = 69

68 − 21 = 47   71 + 19 = 90   50 − 34 = 16   37 + 37 = 74   45 + 24 = 69   29 − 10 = 19

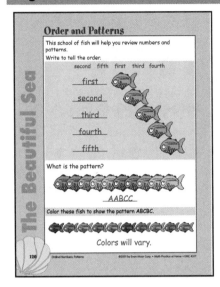

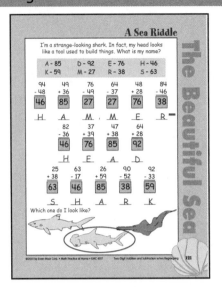

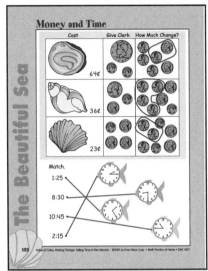

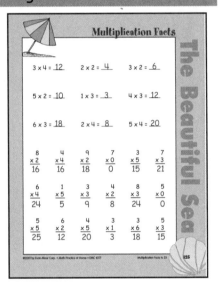

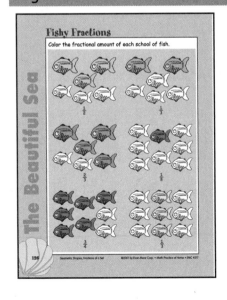

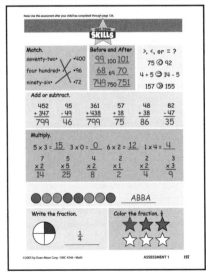

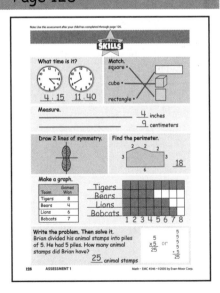

Math • EMC 4546 • ©2005 by Evan-Moor Corp.